CITYSPOTS
FLORE[

Pat Levy

Written by Pat Levy
Original photography by Pat Levy
Front cover photography © Ken Walsh/Getty Images
Series design based on an original concept by Studio 183 Limited

Produced by Cambridge Publishing Management Limited
Project Editor: Catherine Burch
Layout: Julie Crane
Maps: PC Graphics
Transport map: © Communicarta Ltd

Published by Thomas Cook Publishing
A division of Thomas Cook Tour Operations Limited
Company Registration No. 1450464 England
PO Box 227, Unit 18, Coningsby Road
Peterborough PE3 8SB, United Kingdom
email: books@thomascook.com
www.thomascookpublishing.com
+ 44 (0) 1733 416477

ISBN-13: 978-184157-625-1
ISBN-10: 1-84157-625-5

First edition © 2006 Thomas Cook Publishing
Text © 2006 Thomas Cook Publishing
Maps © 2006 Thomas Cook Publishing
Series/Project Editor: Kelly Anne Pipes
Production/DTP: Steven Collins

Printed and bound in Spain by GraphyCems

CONTENTS

SYMBOLS & ABBREVIATIONS

The following symbols are used throughout this book:

ⓐ address **ⓣ** telephone **ⓕ** fax **ⓔ** email **ⓦ** website address
ⓛ opening times **ⓝ** public transport connections **ⓘ** important

The following symbols are used on the maps:

𝒊 information office   O city
✈ airport   O large town
✚ hospital   ○ small town
◎ police station   ▭ motorway
▤ bus station   — main road
▤ railway station   — minor road
Ⓜ metro   — railway
✝ cathedral
❶ numbers denote featured cafés & restaurants

Hotels and restaurants are graded by approximate price as follows:
£ budget **££** mid-range **£££** expensive

▶ *The facade of the Duomo*

Introduction

At times the city of Florence seems as if it has been trapped in a little time bubble – find somewhere high and look over the city, you will see a vista of ancient rooftops, the river snaking away, the Duomo dominating the heart of it. Modern, high rise buildings just don't feature in the city centre and what you see nowadays is pretty much the Florence that Botticelli drank and painted in, where Savonarola lit his bonfire and where Michelangelo left his works in progress for a better offer in Rome. Tucked into medieval buildings are Internet shops, trendy cafés, designer outlets and attractive hotels; grinding its way through streets intended for carts and horses is traffic. Florence has been host to tourists for well over a hundred years and really has the whole tourist industry sorted. You aren't likely to discover amazing antiques at knock down prices but what you will discover is an abundance of the most amazing art, some of it just above your head at street corners or, like Botticelli's St Augustine in Ognissanti, hardly even remarked on by the tour group leader trailing 50 bored teenagers on a morning's cultural appreciation.

But art isn't all you'll find here. Perhaps the restaurants do depend on tourists for their chief source of income but they still produce some excellent, often inexpensive, food. Delicatessen shops fill the city and wonderful breads and cakes tempt the palate. In summer, and pretty much any time of year, Florence's *gelaterie* produce ice cream concoctions of which dreams are made, and *chocolatieres* make chocolate Davids and Duomos to take home... if you have the willpower to keep them that long. Small boutiques by young Italian designers offer fabulous clothes, or you can hang the expense and have a pair of shoes made to your own design.

If it all gets too much, there are Florence's parks to retreat to, or Piazzale Michelangelo high above the city to refresh the spirit and send you back down to the never-ending litany of great masters and wonderful dinners.

🔺 *The clock tower of the Palazzo Vecchio*

When to go

SEASONS & CLIMATE

Inside the museums, every day is a good day regardless of the weather outside. But for those times when you are going to be out and about, you should bear in mind that Florence can have some extremes of weather. From November to around March, temperatures range between −1°C and 15°C (30–59°F) with a high chance of rainfall. Hours of sunshine in these months is about three hours a day. This is the city's low season for tourists so hotel rates are lower, queues are shorter, the restaurants serve some dishes you might be unfamiliar with (game, such as rabbit and boar feature on menus), chestnuts, mushrooms and the new crop of olives will be in the shops. Winter can have some fine cold sunny days, perfect for photography buffs.

As late spring approaches in April and May temperatures begin to rise into the 20s (70s), bringing increased rainfall and humidity. These months are the peak tourist months and so be prepared to queue or pay extra to get into the museums. Temperatures peak in August when many local people abandon the city and take their annual holiday at the seaside. This marks a second low tourist season when you could get some really good last minute bargains at hotels, especially in the upmarket places. In the summer months it is important to be aware of the heat of the sun – wear a hat and sun cream and carry water. It is in these months that you begin to understand Florentine opening hours.

Autumn sees glorious colours in the surrounding countryside and very high humidity in town.

WHEN TO GO ➜

ANNUAL EVENTS
6 January
Befana Rather than Christmas Day, this is the traditional time for children to open their presents. Street parties for children.

PUBLIC HOLIDAYS
During public holidays in Florence most businesses shut, including banks and shops. Restaurants and cafés, however, remain open for the most part. The exception to this is 15 August when even restaurants close. Public transport is restricted on May Day and Christmas Day. When a public holiday falls either side of a weekend – Tuesday or Thursday – most people take off any holiday they are due and enjoy long weekends. Most places shut for a period during July and August. This is arranged on a rota so that there are always places open in each area of the city.

New Year's Day (Capodanno) 1 January
Epiphany (La Befana) 6 January
Easter Monday (Lunedi di Pasqua)
Liberation Day (Venticinque Aprile/Liberazione) 25 April
May Day (Primo Maggio) 1 May
Republic Day (Festa della Repubblica) 2 June
St John's Day (San Giovanni) 24 June
Fest of the Assumption (Ferragosto) 15 August
All Saints' Day (Tutti Santi) 1 November
Festival of the Immaculate Conception
    (Festa dell'Immacolata) 8 December
Christmas Day (Natale) 25 December
St Stephen's Day (Santo Stefano) 26 December

10 days preceding Lent
Carnevale Celebrated in Florence by street processions when children dress up and parade along Lungarno Amerigo Vespucci.

Easter Sunday
Scoppio del Carro A carriage loaded with fireworks is drawn to the doors of the Duomo by white oxen, and a rocket in the shape of a dove is sent from the high altar to ignite it.

1st Sunday after Ascension Sunday (40 days after Easter)
Festa del Grillo (the Cricket Festival) Cricket as in the insect, not the game played with a bat and ball. Stalls and picnics in Cascine Park, where you can buy models of crickets woven from reeds. You might even see real crickets in cages. These are released onto the grass.

May
Maggio Musicale Arts Festival lasting well into June with international performances by orchestras, dance troupes, ballet and lots of fringe events. Events at Teatro Communale, Teatro della Pergola, Palazzo dei Congressi, Teatro Verdi and Bóboli Gardens.

24 (and two other days) June
Calcio in Costume (see page 12)

7 September
Festa della Rificolona Procession of children carrying paper lanterns to celebrate the Virgin Mary's birth. Followed by a parade with floats and street parties.

November–December
Festival dei Popoli Tuscan film festival with films in their original language, with Italian subtitles.
Florence Marathon Starts at Piazzale Michelangelo and finishes at Santa Croce. Participants must be over 18 years of age and have a certificate of health. ☏ 055 5522957 Ⓦ www.firenzemarathon.it

December
Christmas and St Stephen's Day Largely family affairs, but some restaurants do special meals.

🔺 *Easter brings fabulous chocolate creations*

Calcio Storico

In 1530 when foreign troops were besieging the city of Florence and the town was near starvation, just to show their contempt for the enemy, the people of Florence staged an elaborate ball game in full sight of the besieging armies. The city survived and for a few hundred years four teams played out the game each year in

△ *Calcio Storico basically involves mud wrestling in medieval costume*

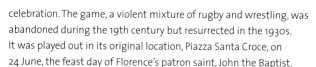

celebration. The game, a violent mixture of rugby and wrestling, was abandoned during the 19th century but resurrected in the 1930s. It was played out in its original location, Piazza Santa Croce, on 24 June, the feast day of Florence's patron saint, John the Baptist.

Since the 1930s the Calcio Storico has become ever more elaborate, with the town's dignitaries wearing full medieval dress, mounted horsemen in full livery, booming cannons, coloured smoke bombs, troops of armed medieval soldiers and drummers and 16 troops of flag jugglers. A ribbon-bedecked white heifer is the prize for the winning team.

The game is simple enough. Two teams of 28 men in their 20s or 30s (without a criminal record) dressed in medieval doublet and hose, attempt to get the heavy leather ball to the far end of the pitch (Piazza Santa Croce, covered in sand for the occasion). Half of them actually run around throwing the ball while the other half engage in some kind of defensive wrestling match designed to prevent the other team from scoring. When a team scores, by reaching their end with the ball and throwing it over the wall erected especially to act as the goal, everyone has hysterics and then the teams change sides and start again. After 50 minutes those left standing with the most goals are the winners. Six referees, also in costume, adjudicate the wrestling aspect of the game. Nowadays you will be pleased to know that the heifer gets a temporary reprieve and returns to its field and the winners get its weight in steak.

Each of the four neighbourhoods of the city put up a team so there are two knockout preliminary games, all played on the Sundays leading up to the 24th. The day ends, after the participants have returned from A&E, with a stupendous firework display from Piazzale Michelangelo.

History

Florence began life in 59 BC as a Roman settlement. It lived long and prospered for about five centuries until the Goths, rampaging across the now dissolute Roman Empire, seized the city, followed in rapid succession by Byzantines, more Goths, Lombards and, finally, Franks. Florence became a small fiefdom ruled over by local, bickering warlords.

Medieval Florence emerged from this economically debilitating period around the 11th century, and in 1115 it and its Tuscan neighbours became independent city states. For a couple of centuries the new and prosperous trades' guilds fought with the old nobility for control of Florence (a bit like the 1980s in Britain, only more bloody and with a different outcome). By the 13th century, the dispute was settled – the trades' guilds were in charge of the Florentine republic and the economy was doing very nicely. Thus began the really big moment in Florentine history – the Renaissance.

As the 15th century began, Florence was one of the biggest and wealthiest cities in Europe. The dominant Medici family, in an effort to placate the Almighty for their use of usury to get very rich, started building churches and commissioning works of art. Renaissance superstars Botticelli, Michelangelo and Donatello dashed off masterpieces from their factories, alongside other objects such as tea trays, headboards (*La Primavera* started off life as a headboard for a Medici bed) and wedding baskets. Humanist thinkers revived ancient Greek and Roman texts, the Church experienced its own Renaissance with the founding of new orders, and science flourished. This all came to an abrupt halt with the death of Lorenzo de Medici and the reactionary ideas of

Savonarola, who burned paintings and manuscripts in a gigantic Bonfire of the Vanities in 1497. The artists decamped to Rome, the economy went into a decline and Florence became a backwater for a few centuries.

In 1864 the various Italian states were unified with Florence as their capital, much to the annoyance of every other big city. Another cultural Renaissance began – not as intense as the last one – and this was the period when the city gained its parks and ring roads. In 1870, Rome replaced Florence as Italy's capital and Florence became a tourist hotspot with Victorians heading there to take in the art, just as we do today.

The next major impact on the city was World War II. Retreating German forces bombed Florence's bridges (sparing Ponte Vecchio) as they left, but that was the worst of the damage. Compared to the rest of Europe, Florence escaped relatively undamaged.

However, what the Allied planes didn't do in 1944, the rain did in 1966 when a huge flood damaged much of what had survived Savonarola. Florence's history since then has been about repairing the damage, dealing with terrible traffic congestion and coming to terms with the euro.

Lifestyle

It would be easy to assume from time spent around the major sights in the city centre that Florence is little more than a tourist draw, trading on the genius of former times. But the people of Florence live quite private and passionate lives. Florentines have adapted themselves to the weather, starting early in the morning with a brief, rushed breakfast and waiting until the middle of the day for the long lunch break, pausing every so often for an espresso. Lunch is a social occasion – no ready-made sandwich from a sandwich bar. Every Florentine has his or her favourite restaurants and dishes, which they gladly share with those tourists who have ventured away from the big piazzas.

With the long lunch comes the late opening. Shops and businesses start to reopen around 15.00 and the streets get more and more lively as families come out to shop, eat or stroll around the city, along the river, through Parco delle Cascine or the gardens leading up to Piazzale Michelangelo.

Dinner is generally eaten later in Florence, which is why so many restaurants have such late opening hours, and meals are relaxed and drawn out – no TV dinners here. After work at the weekend young Florentines like to go to a bar, starting off with aperitifs at their favourite café bar and going on to one of the city's clubs. Sunday is a day for families and the parks fill up with family picnics and football teams practising.

In summer, when the heat and the tourists just get too much, many shops and businesses close down for a fortnight and everyone sensibly goes off to the seaside for a break.

Florentines can come across as a beleaguered lot. Their country appears beset by political scandals, the city is overwhelmed at times by traffic and schemes for traffic improvement (such as the proposed new station), the improvements to the airport and the new metro lines being built, seem to take forever to get underway. In summer the pollution can become so bad that traffic is banned from the city and it is then, and sometimes on Sunday mornings, that you get a sense of what Florence was once like – peaceful narrow streets, hidden gardens and beautifully decorated neighbourhoods.

🔺 *The Italian long lunch*

Culture

THE RENAISSANCE

As long ago as the medieval period, powerful Florentines were commissioning works of art, ranging from cathedrals to beds. Art became an industry with workshops led by a master painter or sculptor, and apprentices learning from them. Much of this medieval art still graces Florence's churches and art galleries – simple representations backed by gold leaf by such men as Cimabue. Change came with artists such as Giotto (1267–1337), who began to paint expressions on the faces of the figures and place them in naturalistic landscapes. At the same time sculptors were studying the classical statuary of ancient Rome and trying to re-create the natural poses and drapery of those works. Artists such as Ghiberti and his apprentice Donatello (1386–1466) began to create naturalistic designs in bronze, such as the Baptistery doors. Donatello went on to create statues standing in naturalistic poses, such as the bronze David, and the St George, now in the Bargello, their faces full of character. These sculptors prompted painters such as Masaccio, who discovered the use of perspective, and then came Fra Angelico who put all these new ideas into his paintings in the monastery of San Marco (now the museum). Fra Angelico's simple figures move naturally, live in a real landscape and their faces carry emotional depth.

Artists continued the idea of real figures and started adding their employers' faces, sitting rooms and palaces to their paintings. The Medici are all over the city, as the Magi, as figures ascending to heaven, as fashionably dressed attendants to the birth of Jesus in a Florentine bedroom.

> *Giambologna's* Rape of the Sabine Women, *in Piazza della Signoria*

Filippo Lippi wanted none of this. A Carmelite friar and the teacher of Sandro Botticelli, he painted fantastical landscapes full of symbolism and flat, one-dimensional faces looking straight out at you. Botticelli took up his ideas, creating allegorical figures whose feet seem to float above the imaginary landscape around them.

Fifteenth-century Florence was an exciting place to be. The city's economy and its writers, painters, architects and philosophers all made Florence a model of Renaissance culture. Leonardo da Vinci (1452–1519), was a prolific painter, architect and sculptor, but he also explored the world of invention and the study of anatomy and nature. Michelangelo stunned the world with his mammoth yet delicate statue *David*, now housed in the Accademia.

Mannerism was a reaction against the naturalism of Renaissance art, with highly stylised, brightly coloured, unnaturally shaped figures and scenes. This can be seen in the work of Andrea del Sarto (1486–1530), for example his *Madonna of the Harpies* in the Uffizi, or in the work of Vasari (1511–74), whose Mannerist frescoes decorate the dome of the Duomo.

With so much art to admire, it could seem there is little time for anything else in Florence, but this would be a pity. Florence has several theatres which run full programmes of theatre, chamber music, opera and classical and modern dance. Contemporary artists are doing well and their works can be seen in private galleries around the city.

Quarter Modern art gallery partly private and part public. Outside the city gates. Ⓐ Viale Giannotti 81 ☎ 055 6802555 🕐 16.00–20.00 Tues–Sun Ⓝ Bus: 23

▶ *Picturesque mementos*

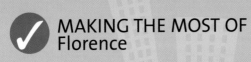

MAKING THE MOST OF
Florence

Shopping

Almost as big a draw as the Uffizi are Florence's shops, which are still small, family-run businesses, craft workshops and markets. All the big name Italian designers have branches here – Versace, Gucci, Armani, Ferragamo, Prada – as well as French designers, and there are some good local department stores. Even better, this shopping heaven lies in a compact area of the inner city so you don't have to take the bus out to an anonymous out-of-town shopping centre to find good things.

While tiny, gorgeous shops lurk around every corner there are certain areas of town where you might best direct your attention. The designer shops can be found in Via de'Tornabuoni and Via della Vigna Nuova. Oltrarno has lots of workshops where traditional crafts are still carried out, while Via Maggio and Via dei Fossi focus on antiques. Ponte Vecchio is, of course, the bridge for jewellery while San Lorenzo market has the traditional taking-home-a-gift-for-the-in-laws stuff. If, however, you need the whole shopping centre experience, head out to the unimaginatively named The Mall, about 30 minutes out of the city, where the designers have their factory outlets.

Shoe lovers will enjoy Florence. Besides the aforementioned big names there are also tiny shops making beautiful footwear from Tuscan leather. Bags, belts, gloves and clothing, too, are handcrafted in the city, and the best place to look is around the streets adjoining Piazza Santa Croce or San Lorenzo market.

There are a few things that visitors might find unusual while shopping in Florence, especially in the smaller shops. The sign *entrata libera* outside the shop means that you are welcome to browse with no compulsion to buy. Traditionally if you go into a shop you are expected to announce what you are looking for and be shown examples of it. The sign indicates that you will not be expected to do this. Another strange custom are the hours of opening (see page 145). Lots of small shops and the markets close completely for a period during the holiday months of July and August while the family goes off on holiday, so be prepared.

USEFUL SHOPPING PHRASES

What time do the shops open/close?
A che ora aprono/chiudono i negozi?
Ah keh awra ahprawnaw/kewdawnaw ee nehgotsee?

How much is this?
Quant' è?
Kwahnteh?

Can I try this on?
Posso provarlo?
Pawssaw prawvarrlaw?

My size is ...
La mia taglia è ...
Lah meeyah tahlyah eh ...

I'll take this one, thank you.
Prenderò questo, grazie.
Prehndehroh kwestaw, grahtsyeh.

Can you show me the one in the window/this one?
Può mostrarmi quello in vetrina/questo?
Pooh oh mawstrahrmee kwehllaw een vehtreenah/kwehstaw?

This is too large/too small/too expensive.
Questo è troppo grande/troppo piccolo/troppo caro.
*Kwestaw eh tropaw grahndeh/tropaw peekawlaw/
trawpaw kahraw.*

Eating & drinking

WHAT'S IN A NAME?

Restaurants in Florence go by many names – *trattoria, osteria, ristorante, rosticceria, tavola calda, gelaterie, pizzeria*. Generally speaking, the name denotes the aspirations of the owner rather than what food you will find inside. *Trattoria* are generally more casual than *osteria* or *ristorante*, although none of them demand black tie and tails. *Pizzeria* will indubitably have similar things on their menus to the others but will be slightly downmarket and cheaper. *Rosticceria* will include a grill and serve grilled meat along with the other standard dishes, often to take out as well as eat inside. Having *tavola calda* in the name generally indicates that the place is open at lunchtime both for hot dishes, such as pastas, and cold cooked dishes to eat in or take out. Besides these variations there are café bars which offer a range of foods, from ready-cooked pastas, filled rolls, toasted breads and cakes.

Generally if these places have a bar the food will cost less if you eat it standing at the bar than if you take a table. You will notice scales on the counter. Food such as pastas, pizza or focaccia will be sold to you by weight. Occasionally you tell the cashier what you want and pay for it, and then take the bill to the counter.

MENUS
Antipasto

This may be a plate of cured meat with bread, possibly boar (*cinghiale*) salami, prosciutto, or chicken liver paté, served with *crostini*, tiny pieces of toasted or fried bread.

Primo

The first course will consist of pasta, risotto or soup. Other dishes to try on this course are *panzanella*, a mixture of white bread soaked in water with herbs, beans, raw onion and tomatoes. *Bruschetta* also appears in this course. Sauces for pasta are often made with game – rabbit or hare, boar or pigeon. Ravioli made with pear and pecorino cheese is a Florentine speciality.

Secondo

The main course is predominantly meat-based, especially in winter. Warming stews of spiced rabbit or boar are typical, while in warmer months T-bone steak cooked very very rare, called *bistecca fiorentina*, is served for two or three people. Fish, if it is on the menu, will appear in this course.

Contorno

An accompanying vegetable dish might be white beans tossed in oil, globe artichoke, boiled potatoes served with capers and oil and pepper, or any one of a variety of salads, using wild rocket, radicchio, or even globe artichokes served raw.

Fruta, formaggio, dolce

After the main course there are choices of cheese – often *pecorino*, the Tuscan cheese made from sheep's milk – some fresh fruit or a dessert, such as *panforte*, a thick jaw-gluing fruit cake. Tiramisu is not native but appears on menus. Finish the meal with an espresso.

❶ You should note that smoking is not allowed in restaurants (or any public places) unless there is a dedicated room for non-smokers.

Drinking

Tuscany is a major producer of both red and white wine. The most famous of these is Chianti, the best of it from Ruffina or Classico. In recent years, wine growers have introduced French grapes to Tuscan vineyards and Tuscan wine has become so complex that now *il turismo enogastronomico* is an entire industry, with visitors touring the vineyards of Tuscany and tasting the wines (ⓦ www.movimentotourismovino.it).

Aperitifs are often Campari or Cinzano; to end a meal, a digestif might be grappa, or a sweet liqueur such as amaro or limoncello.

Coffee

Coffee drinking in Florence comes with certain rules. Cappuccino is drunk only in the morning with breakfast, and is usually served lukewarm. Espresso is drunk during the day, often with a shot of spirits. Other coffee options are caffé Americano – espresso diluted with water to make a normal size coffee, or caffé macchiato – espresso with milk or foam added.

Vegetarians

Eating out isn't too bad for vegetarians. Check the pasta courses first as well as the salads and vegetable accompaniments. Some excellent pizza options are purely vegetarian. There are Middle Eastern fast food places offering falafel, and two dedicated restaurants.

PRICE RATING
Restaurant categories are based on a three-course meal for one person, without drinks.
£ less than €22; ££ €22–€40; £££ more than €40

Il Vegetariano £ Lots of ethnic choices, a salad bar, rustic cookery.
📍 Via delle Ruote 30r ☎ 055 475030 🕐 12.30–14.30, 19.30–22.30
Tues–Fri, evenings only Sat & Sun (see map page 83)

Ruth's £ Kosher fish and vegetable-based dishes. Lots of Middle
Eastern dishes, meze, couscous, pastas and salads. 📍 Via Farini 2A
☎ 055 2480888 🕐 12.30–14.30, 20.00–22.00 Mon–Thur, lunch only Fri
(see map page 59)

USEFUL DINING PHRASES

I would like a table for ... people.
Vorrei un tavolo per ... persone.
Vawrray oon tahvawlaw perr ... perrsawneh.

Waiter/waitress!
Cameriere/cameriera!
Cahmehryereh/cahmehryera!

May I have the bill, please?
Mi dà il conto, per favore?
Mee dah eel cawntaw, perr fahvawreh?

Could I have it well-cooked/medium/rare please?
Potrei averlo ben cotto/mediamente cotto/poco cotto, per favore?
Pawtray ahvehrlaw behn cawtaw/mehdeeyahmehnteh cawtaw/pawcaw cawtaw perr fahvawreh?

I am a vegetarian. Does this contain meat?
Sono vegetariano/vegetariana (fem.). Contiene carne?
Sawnaw vejetahreeahnaw/vejetahreeahnah. Contyehneh kahrneh?

Entertainment & nightlife

Florence may not be on the must-do-a-gig list of the really big names in entertainment, but it has a thriving nightlife. For visitors there are lots of get-out-of your-brain pubs serving canned British beers with special offers on shots, no entry charge and really loud music. There are flyers around the city in the station, record shops and in hotels, giving details of what music is on which nights. The middle of the week is often good if you are female. For the more discerning, the city's cafés metamorphose at night into bars, serving *aperitivo* – little snacks free with the drinks early in the evening, in the hope that punters stay for the night.

The city's clubs have metamorphosed in recent years. Like the café bars they serve food during the day, changing at night into cleverly lit, stylish places offering cosy seating areas and chill out rooms. In summer clubs, like bars and restaurants, find an outside space to operate in, changing every year as different spaces, especially along the river, in the piazzas or the park, get permission to open up. Check with *The Florentine*, the English language paper, or *Firenze Specttacolo*.

Live music is available in the city, with jazz and Latin American music a regular feature. Venues for the really big shows are all out of the city centre – Palasport Mandela Forum is where the big tours usually go to, while the smaller Saschall-Teatro di Firenze has lesser events. Tickets for both are available from Box Office (see below). Sala Vanni in Piazza del Carmine, Oltrarno (ⓦ www.musicusconcentus.com) often plays host to jazz and classical performances. Occasionally the football stadium

ⓓ *The magic of Florence by night*

accommodates the really big megastars. Smaller places which have regular live music include the Astor Café (see page 97), BZF (page 97) and Girasol (🅐 Via del Romito 1, outside the city gates ☎ 055 474948 🅦 www.girasol.it 🕒 20.00–02.30 Tues–Sun). Girasol is predominantly Latin American, and Jazz Club (see page 71) has live jazz nightly. In summer there are open air jazz sessions in Piazza della Santissima Annunziata (🅦 www.firenzejazz.it). In Oltrarno, Caffè la Torre (page 110) has a wide range of live music most nights.

Classical music thrives in Florence, opera having been invented there, or so the story goes. There are regular opera performances in the city at Teatro del Maggio Musicale Fiorentino and Teatro Goldini in Oltrarno, while the Lutheran Church (🅐 Lungarno Torrigiani 11) has regular, free organ and chamber music. Tickets for opera performances from Box Office (see below).

The theatre is obviously generally aimed at Italian speakers, so it can be difficult for visitors. Most productions take place between September and April. Dance has a more international appeal, and performances of ballet and modern dance take place regularly at the Teatro del Maggio. Films in Florence, like television, are for the

TICKETS
Teatro della Pergola 🅐 Via della pergola 12–13, San Marco ☎ 055 2264316 🅦 www.pergola.firenze.it Visiting theatre productions.
MaggioDanza ☎ 055 213535 🅦 www.maggiofiorentino.com Classical and modern ballet productions.
Box Office 🅐 Via Alammani 39, Santa Maria Novella ☎ 055 210804 🅦 www.box.it 🕒 10.00–19.30 Mon–Sat. Tickets for most productions in the city.

most part dubbed into Italian, although Odeon Original Sound,
a beautiful art nouveau cinema, shows English language films two
or three times a week, occasionally before they are premiered
in Britain. These may be dubbed and subtitled in English.
ⓐ Via Sassetti 1 ① 055 214068 ⓦ www.cinehall.it. Cinecittà
occasionally has English language or subtitled movies but you must
have a membership card. ⓐ Via Bacchio da Montelupo 35 (outside
the city gates) ① 055 7324510

⬤ The romantic city

Sport & relaxation

Florence isn't the first place that comes to mind when planning a sporting holiday, but there are active things to do around the city, including the annual marathon. Just walking up to Piazzale Michelangelo may be enough exertion for one day, especially in the summer, but for the more energetic, here is the sport on offer.

SPECTATOR SPORTS
Football
Stadio Artemio Franchi is the home of Florence's football team, Fiorentina. Games are played between August and May, usually every other Sunday. Tickets can be bought online or at the stadium.
ⓐ Campo di Marte (outside the city gates) ⓘ 055 2625537
ⓦ www.acffiorentina.it Ⓝ Bus: 11, 17

Horse racing
Ippodrome delle Cascine is based in Cascine Park, outside the city gates, and regularly holds flat race meetings. Early in the morning the horses are put through their paces in the park, if you just like looking at horses. ⓐ Via delle Cascine 3, Parco delle Cascine
ⓘ 055 4226076 ⓦ www.ippodromifiorentini.it Ⓛ Apr–May, Sept–Oct
Ⓝ Bus: 17c

Motor racing
Autodromo del Mugello, 30 km (19 miles) north of the city, is a prominent feature in the world of motor sport, and regular meetings are held here. On the quiet days motor cycle addicts can bring their bike and try out the circuit. ⓘ 055 8499111
ⓦ www.mugellocircuit.it Ⓛ Mar–Nov

PARTICIPATION SPORTS

Skate hire

Skates can be hired from **Le Pavoniere** in Cascine Park. ⓐ Viale della Catena 2, Parco dell Cascine ⓣ 335 5718547 ⓛ 15.00–20.00 Tues–Thur, 10.00–20.00 Sat & Sun ⓝ Bus: 17C

Squash

Centro Squash Firenze Squash courts, gym, sauna and equipment hire. ⓐ Via Empoli 16, San Quirico ⓣ 055 7323055 ⓛ 09.30–23.00 Mon–Fri, 09.30–18.00 Sat ⓝ Bus: 1

Swimming

Piscina Bellariva Set in a park to the east of the city, this is an Olympic-size pool. Smaller pool for children. ⓐ Lungarno Aldo Moro 6 (outside the city gates) ⓣ 055 677521 ⓛ 10.00–18.00 Mon–Wed, Fri–Sun, 10.00–18.00, 20.30–23.30 Tues & Thur

Trekking & walking

Gruppo Escursionistico Club Alpino Italiano organise treks through the Tuscan hills on Sundays. ⓐ Via del Mezzetta 2 (outside the city gates) ⓣ 055 6120467 ⓦ www.caifirenze.it

Walking Tours of Florence offer a range of walking tours of the city, arranging entry to museums and meals as well as bicycle tours of Tuscany. ⓐ Piazza Santa Stefano 2 ⓣ 055 2645033 ⓦ www.italy.artviva.com ⓛ 08.00–18.30 Mon–Sat, mornings only Sun

Accommodation

There are various official categories of accommodation in Florence, ranging from the 5 star ratings for hotels, to B&Bs. To be classed as a hotel and get a star rating, an establishment must have seven or more rooms. Smaller places than this are *affitacamere* (rooms for rent), which can be anything from a B&B to just that – a room in someone's house. *Residenza d'epoca* is a B&B in a listed building. Confusingly a *Residence* is accommodation which is chiefly self-catering apartments.

There are vast numbers of hotels in the city, with many of the larger 2- and 3-star places catering for tour groups. This may be all very well, but if the place is small there can be problems when groups come and go in a day or so. Everyone gets up at the same time (and gets back from their day's tour at the same time) and hot water and breakfast can be at a premium.

The peak season for visiting the city starts around late March and goes on until July. Booking hotels at that time can be difficult, and will cost more than in the low season. In the very hot months of late July and August, prices can fall again sharply, often like budget airline prices, rising and falling with demand. If a place has low occupancy and you turn up late in the afternoon, you may get a sizeable discount. Demand, and price, go up again in September.

PRICE RATINGS
The following are based on the price per night of double occupancy with breakfast.
£ up to €100; ££ €100–€250; £££ over €250

▶ *Florence, the city of EM Forster's* A Room With a View

Camping Michelangelo £ Close to Piazzale Michelangelo, this campsite is close to town and has amazing views. Bring your own tent or hire a 'house tent' with beds. There is a bar, restaurant, supermarket and disco. Be prepared, though, as it can get crowded and noisy in the summer. ⓐ Viale Michelangelo 80 ⓣ 055 6811977 Ⓝ Bus: 12, 13

Hotel de la Pace £ Medium-sized hotel in what was once a *palazzo*. Rooms are fair sized and have a modern en suite bathroom, TV and mini-bar. There is lots of public space and a pleasant breakfast room. Things can get a little run down here, with tour groups passing through every couple of days. OK if you can avoid the big traffic flow through the breakfast room. ⓐ Via Lamamora 28 ⓣ 055 577343

Hotel Orchidea £ The house that Dante's Beatrice was born in has got to be a good place to stay. Simple rooms, mostly not en suite but hand basins in the rooms. Very inexpensive. ⓐ Borgo degli Albizi 11 ⓣ 055 2480346 Ⓦ www.hotelorchideaflorence.it

Residenza Johanna Uno £ Excellent value in this well-run, small and cosy B&B, close to San Marco. ⓐ Via Bonifacio Lupi 14 ⓣ 055 481896 Ⓦ www.johanna.it

Residenza Johlea Uno £ More good value from the same people as Johanna Uno. Comfortable and roomy. Ⓛ Via San Gallo 80 ⓣ 055 4633292 Ⓦ www.johanna.it

Annalena ££ Small 3-star hotel in a quiet area, south of Palazzo Pitti. Antiques, a garden and thoughtful staff make this a serious alternative to city centre hotels. ⓐ Via Romana 34 ⓣ 055 222402 ⓦ www.hotelannalena.it

Belletini ££ 27 rooms, 2-star – too small for tour groups, which is always a good sign. All rooms have air conditioning, some have TVs and private bathrooms. Great breakfast. ⓐ Via dei Conti 7 ⓣ 055 213561 ⓦ www.firenze.net/hotelbelletini

Casci ££ Friendly small hotel in a 15th-century *palazzo* with lots of reading material, an open plan bar and breakfast room, plus simple but well-maintained bedrooms. ⓐ Via Cavour 13 ⓣ 055 211686 ⓦ www.hotelcasci.com

Morandi alla Crocetta ££ Small, friendly 3-star hotel, run by English-speaking staff. Pleasant rooms, some with original medieval frescoes, antiques and views over the garden. ⓐ Via Laura 50 ⓣ 055 2344747 ⓦ www.hotelmorandi.it

Relais Grand Tour ££ Each room is individually styled in this pretty B&B in a 16th-century house. Suites are more expensive but worth the luxury. TV on request. ⓐ Via Santa Reparata 21 ⓣ 055 283955 ⓦ www.florencegrandtour.com

Residenza d'Epoca in Piazza della Signoria ££ Graceful B&B with lots of public space, comprising ten individually designed rooms, many overlooking the piazza, and three apartments. Breakfast is a shared table or can be eaten privately in your room. Enjoy internet use for guests, hot water always on tap for hot drinks and lots of friendly advice and assistance. ⓐ Via dei Magazzini 2 ⓣ 055 2399546 ⓦ www.inpiazzadellasignoria.it

Grand Hotel Minerva £££ Conveniently located in Piazza Santa Maria Novella this modern-looking, bright hotel has comfortable rooms with kettles (there are very few places with this facility in town), views over the piazza or over the church, and a small pool and bar on the roof. In summer the restaurant moves out to the piazza. ⓐ Piazza Santa Maria Novella 16 ⓣ 055 26828 ⓦ www.grandhotelminerva.com

Grand Hotel Villa Medici £££ A very special place where you are really pampered. The hotel is in an 18th-century villa with private grounds and decorated with antiques. Rooms have all mod cons imaginable, including some with whirlpools and balconies, which can be a godsend in summer. The hotel has a pool and is just outside the city walls, behind Santa Maria Novella. There is also a glorious buffet breakfast. ⓐ Via Il Prato 42 ⓣ 055 277171 ⓦ www.villamedicihotel.com

Villa La Vedetta £££ Extreme luxury on the top of Viale Michelangelo. This hotel, recently converted from two private villas, is set in its own gardens, with two pools, and the most amazing views in the city. There is a fitness room and sauna, and every convenience in the guest rooms, including Internet connection via the flat screen TV. ⓐ Viale Michelangelo 78 ⓣ 055 238531 ⓦ www.concertohotels.com

ⓞ *For luxury, you can't beat Villa La Vedetta*

THE BEST OF FLORENCE

Whether you are on a flying visit to Florence or taking a more
leisurely break in northern Italy, the city and its surroundings
offer some sights, places and experiences that should not
be missed.

TOP 10 ATTRACTIONS

- **The Uffizi** Home to some of the most moving and beautiful
  artwork in the world (see page 63).

- **The Duomo** Because size matters (see page 84).

- **Santa Maria Novella** For the beautiful Renaissance frescoes
  (see page 77).

- **San Marco** Where Savonarola lived and where Fra Angelico's
  beautiful paintings still have their original simplicity and
  intensity (see page 92).

- **Ponte Vecchio** Where all that glisters probably is gold
  (see page 74).

- **Walking or cycling tour of the city** Get the feel of the medieval streets beneath your feet in the company of a guide who knows the city well (see page 33).

- **Mercato Centrale** Where you can buy anything from a whole pecorino cheese to a new leather outfit (see page 95).

- **Michelangelo's *David*** A living, passionate creature carved from an inanimate piece of marble (see page 90).

- **Piazzale Michelangelo** Get out of town, enjoy the fresh air and admire the views of the whole city (see page 102).

- **A night on the town** Start off with aperitifs in **Dolce Vita** (page 110) and work your way back to town, ending up at **Jazz Club** (page 71) for some soothing jazz.

⬇ *The Ponte Vecchio and River Arno*

Your at-a-glance guide to seeing the best Florence has to offer, depending on how much time you have. It's a small city, so it's not hard to get a good feel for it in a short visit.

HALF-DAY: FLORENCE IN A HURRY

Book in advance to get priority entrance to the Uffizi. You haven't got time to dally, so just go straight to the *Primavera* and the *Birth of Venus*, check out the Michelangelos and on the way out have a quick look at Titian's *Urbino Venus*. Head out to Mercato Nuovo to touch *Il Porcellino*'s, nose (a bronze boar), for luck, then buy some tourist items. Then swing south to the Ponte Vecchio, where you can admire or even buy some of the jewellery. Get a cab up to Piazzale Michelangelo and take your camera.

ONE DAY: TIME TO SEE A LITTLE MORE

Spend a little longer in the Uffizi – after all you've shelled out a small fortune to get in there. Pre-book the Accademia and go and marvel at *David*, taking in Michelangelo's other works. Lunch at Rivoire in Piazza della Signoria or one of the cafés in Piazza della Repubblica – the people-watching is great fun. In the afternoon check out the market and Ponte Vecchio, and head on to Palazzo Pitti to wonder at the brash riches of the Medici. As dusk approaches, enjoy the cool of the evening with a walk across Ponte alle Grazie and join the crowds taking photos of Ponte Vecchio with the setting sun behind it. Walk quickly up to Piazzale Michelangelo to take in the gorgeous nightscapes and end with a meal at Florence's only Michelin-starred restaurant, Onice (page 109), or any of the many atmospheric cafés.

2–3 DAYS: SHORT CITY BREAK

In two or three days there is time to relax and enjoy the sights listed earlier. Joining the queues, rather than paying extra to get in the museums, becomes a possibility. You can have some fascinating experiences while queuing at the Uffizi. Add the Bargello to your list of museums and check out San Marco, San Lorenzo and Santa Croce. The Museo Leonardo da Vinci makes a pleasant change from all the art, and you can explore some of the small streets around Santa Croce and the Mercato Centrale, checking out the leather workshops and restaurants. The streets between the Duomo, the river and the railway station are filled with gorgeous little shops so spend at least an early evening shopping.

LONGER: ENJOYING FLORENCE TO THE FULL

With longer in the city, you can put away the map and begin to look like a local. There is time to get out for a proper exploration of Oltrarno, the Bóboli Gardens, the weird museum La Specola and enjoy dinner in one of the piazzas on the south side of the river. Consider a day trip to Siena for its medieval feel and quieter atmosphere. Take in Pisa and laugh at the people posing for the funny shot holding up the tower. If you're not overdosed on art, seek out some of the smaller churches – Ognissanti or Orsanmichele.

Something for nothing

Things can be expensive in Florence. Most museums have an entrance fee and some have a fee for queue jumping added on! Even churches charge quite high entrance fees to go inside, which might seem a bit unchristian but they do have high costs in upkeep. But there are things for free in the city. Window shopping is one inexpensive way to spend an afternoon, but it requires great willpower. The views from Piazzale Michelangelo are completely free, as is the walk through pleasant parkland up to it. Entrance to Parco delle Cascine is also free and there are football matches and people to watch. A stroll along the river in the cool of the evening is a popular activity in Florence and also costs nothing. The city's markets are an experience in themselves, and touching the bronze boar for luck in Mercato Nuovo is free. Many important artworks are in the city streets and can be viewed at no expense. Look up at street corners to see frescoes and other shrines put there hundreds of years ago by the city's various guilds. Piazza della Signoria provides a home for an amazing collection of statuary.

The following do not charge an entrance fee:

Biblioteca Medicea-Laurenziana Library built to hold the Medici manuscripts with a staircase designed by Michelangelo (page 88).

Cloisters of Spedale degli Innocenti (page 89).

Ognissanti Amazing atmosphere and a Botticelli (page 74).

Orsanmichele Beautiful exterior and elaborate tabernacle inside. Next door is the Museo do Orsanmichele, also free and full of statues removed from the exterior. @ Via dell'Arte della Lana ● 055 28494 ● 09.00–12.00, 16.00–18.00

San Miniato al Monte A lovely church with spectacular views over the city (page 102).

Santa Felicità (page 105).

Santissima Annunciata Church with a painting finished by an angel (page 89).

Santa Trinità A 13th-century church, whose highlight is the Cappella Sassetti covered in frescoes by Ghirlandaio. One of these is set in the Piazza della Signoria and includes portraits of Lorenzo the Magnificent and his children (page 75).

Santo Spirito A fine church with frescoes by Filippino Lippi (page 102).

🔺 *The green and white inlaid marble facade of San Miniato al Monte*

When it rains

The city's narrow streets can occasionally make a rainy day seem like a battle ground. There is rarely room for two umbrella-wielding pedestrians to pass, and dodging umbrella spikes can be quite

◢ *The Uffizi offers hours of indoor entertainment*

dangerous. It's lucky then that so much of what people come to see in the city is indoors.

A good place to be in a queue in the rain is at the Uffizi where the queue stands under a loggia and is entertained for hours by buskers and pavement artists. Not so the Accademia, where queuing in the rain can be a misery. The Uffizi has the added bonus of an amazing series of shops selling very tasteful versions of the artworks – *Primavera* jigsaws, Rembrandt coffee mugs, *Urbino Venus* plastic aprons as well as some excellent books, beautiful shawls and even some jewellery modelled on designs in some of the more famous paintings.

The Uffizi has another advantage – you are inside for so long (making sure the queuing was worth it) that by the time you come out it's time to slink off to a café and watch the rain from inside.

Finding one of the cinemas that does English language films (see page 31) is a good option on a rainy day, while sitting under the protective canopy at Rivoire (page 67) or one of the other cafés drinking hot chocolate and watching other people getting wet is a pleasant experience. The Bargello is another good place to visit when it rains. The queues are much smaller here and the lobby holds most of the people who want to buy a ticket. Its inner courtyard is open to the sky but the route between the rooms is covered. Really looking at the collection of statuary in each of the rooms takes a long time and what better opportunity to do that than when you don't want to go out in the rain. You can also spend the time eavesdropping on the guides taking the tour groups around – you learn a lot about what you are looking at that way.

Finally, if it is summer and temperatures have been up in the 40s (100s), it's quite pleasant to just go outside and get wet.

On arrival

ARRIVING

By air

Most travellers will arrive on a short visit to the city by plane,
arriving at Pisa International Airport and taking the train or bus into
Florence. Florence has its own airport but there are very few
connections to the UK.

Pisa Galileo Galilei Airport (☎ 050 849111 ⓦ www.pisa-airport.com)

The airport is connected by direct rail link to Santa Maria Novella
station. Trains run hourly and journey time is a little over an hour.
Trains stop at about 22.00. Pisa has a second railway station, some
distance from the airport, where trains run later but journey time is
twice as long.

The alternative is the Terravison bus run by Ryanair from the
airport parking lot. Tickets are available in the main concourse and
cost the same as the train, taking a few minutes longer in journey
time. Buses run irregularly, and the timetable is geared to the arrival
times of flights so that there are late buses if there is a late flight.
Use of the bus is not restricted to Ryanair passengers. The bus
arrives at Santa Maria Novella station and continues on to Florence
Airport. ⓦ www.lowcostcoach.com

Aeroporto di Firenze (ⓐ Amerigo Vespucci ☎ 055 30615
ⓦ www.aeroporto.firenze.it)

Many people are aware that air travel emits CO_2, which
contributes to climate change. You may be interested in the
possibility of lessening the environmental impact of your flight
through the charity Climate Care, which offsets your CO_2 by
funding environmental projects around the world. Visit
www.climatecare.org

The airport is about 5 km (3 miles) west of the city centre, linked to the city by Volainbus, running half hourly from 06.00–23.30 and arriving at the SITA bus station at Santa Caterina da Siena. Taxis are more expensive and take about 25 minutes.

By train

Santa Maria Novella (☎ 055 2352061 🕐 04.15–01.30, Information office 07.00–21.00; Ticket office 05.50–22.00)

The station is located in the west side of the city centre. From here taxis are the best bet, or buses 12 and 13 follow a circular route from Santa Maria Novella through Piazza della Libertà, across town to Piazzale Michelangelo.

By road

Traffic in the city centre is severely limited during the daytime to public transport and permit holders, although hire cars are allowed to drive to the hotels. In summer, when the pollution levels get high, traffic is banned in some areas of the city altogether. Digital signs along the inbound roads indicate these bans, which can change from one day to the next and at short notice. If you intend to bring a car to the city or hire one, choose a hotel outside of the restricted zone and be prepared to pay high parking fees.

FINDING YOUR FEET

Florence can be a confusing city at first. Its street plan was laid out in medieval times and roads that you think are going in one direction can often take you somewhere you never intended. It is a good idea to think of the city in terms of its major churches. Taking the Duomo as the central focal point (it's a bit hard to miss, even several streets away), Via Calzaiuoli runs directly south towards

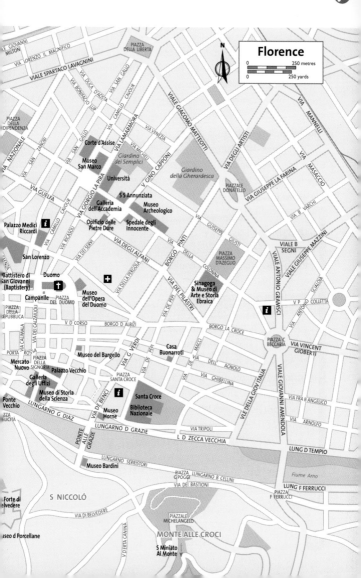

Piazza della Signoria which leads on to the river. Westwards from the Duomo, Via de' Cerretani leads towards Piazza di Santa Maria Novella and the railway station. East from the Duomo, roads wander southwards towards Piazza Santa Croce. Finally north from the Duomo, the roads lead up to San Marco and San Lorenzo. South of the river is Oltrarno and the Palazzo Pitti. The tourist office and most hotels supply free city maps which indicate the major sights.

Two things that visitors from the UK should be aware of are that the traffic drives on the right side of the road and that pedestrian crossings do not have the same rules as those in the UK. What looks like a zebra crossing is in fact a suggestion that you might like to try

IF YOU GET LOST, TRY ...

Excuse me, do you speak English?
Mi scusi, parla inglese?
Mee scoozee, parrla eenglehzeh?

Excuse me, is this the right way to the old town/the city centre/the tourist office/ the station/the bus station?
Mi scusi, è questa la strada per città vecchia/al centro città/l'ufficio informazioni turistiche/alla stazione ferroviaria/ alla stazione degli autobus?
Mee scoozee, eh kwehstah lah strahda perr lah cheetta vehkyah/ahl chentraw cheetteh/looffeechaw eenforrmahtsyawnee tooreesteekeh/ahlla stahtsyawneh ferrawvyarya/ahlla stahtsyawneh delee ahootawboos?

▶ *The Neptune Fountain, Piazza della Signoria*

your luck crossing at that point, but don't expect anyone to do anything more than swerve in order to miss hitting you. Secondly the sacred British green man signal (in Florence the word Avanti in green) still doesn't mean you are entirely safe, since traffic turning into the road can ignore it.

There are no areas where you should be particularly concerned about safety in the city, although like all other cities it has its dangers. In the past, Piazza Santa Maria Novella was a little on the seedy side but with the flash new hotels opening in the area this is no longer the case. The area around the railway station can be a bit fraught, with lots of street people hanging around into the early hours.

GETTING AROUND

Florence is such a small city that there is hardly any need for public transport. Buses 12 and 13 make a circuit of the city and are useful for getting to Oltrarno and Piazzale Michelangelo. Number 7 travels from Santa Maria Novella to Piazza San Marco and then north out of town. In addition there are four electric bus services which do smaller circuits of the city:

A travels from east to west of the city, from Piazza Santa Maria Novella through Via Vigna Nuova, Via de Tornabuoni around the Duomo and then west along Via Ghibellina and back along Borgo degli Albizi.

B follows the river from Santa Croce to Via de'Fossi and back along a more northerly route.

C travels around the east of the city.

D travels around Oltrarno.

Tickets for these buses can be bought from news stands, bars or tobacconists displaying the bus company sign (ATAF). Tickets only

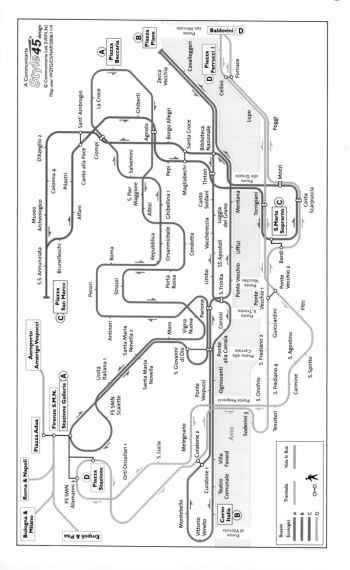

become valid when they are stamped in the machine at the front of the bus and last three hours, so they can be used for a second or third journey if it is within the time limit. It is possible to buy multiple journey tickets which last two or three days, but these are unlikely to be useful in such a small city. Buses run from about 05.30–21.00 every 10–30 minutes. Don't depend on timetables at the bus stops – traffic in the city will ruin the best laid plans of the bus companies.

A night bus, the number 70, operates all night. It leaves Santa Maria Novella station and heads into the city centre, then travels north to Campo di Marte and back to Santa Maria Novella.

Taxis are white and cannot be flagged down in the street. You must find a cab rank or phone for one. When you phone you will be given a code name and a number which will be on the door of the cab. The minimum fare is €3.65, and the fare increases by 70c per km or period of waiting. Calling a cab has a surcharge of €1.71 and there is another charge for each piece of luggage. The meter is turned on as soon as the call is made to the taxi company so there may be some euros on the meter when the cab picks you up.

Taxi ranks are indicated by a blue sign. Ranks are in Piazza della Repubblica, Piazza della Stazione, Piazza Santa Maria Novella, Piazza del Duomo, Piazza San Marco, Piazza Santa Croce and Piazza di Santa Trinità. Taxis are easy to come by in the low tourist season but can be difficult to find in the summer.

◐ *One of the many elaborate details on Orsanmichele*

The Uffizi & East

This is the tourist heart of Florence, with Piazza della Signoria at its centre. Tourists here easily outnumber locals and you will spend your time dodging long crocodiles of bored teenagers led by irritated teachers and miked-up tour guides waving umbrellas. Street artists, men painted silver and musicians all compete with the museums to relieve you of your cash. Everything here is dedicated to the tourist industry, but much of it does a good job and as you wander through the Uffizi or the Bargello, encountering so many icons of Western culture, you cannot fail to be moved by the majesty of it all. Restaurants abound here, lots of them in the little streets snaking eastwards past Santa Croce. Or you may prefer to seek out Standa, in Via Pietrapiana – a huge supermarket with an excellent bakery, ideal for stocking up on essentials, such as cold meats, wine and fruit, for a simple picnic lunch.

SIGHTS & ATTRACTIONS

Palazzo Vecchio

Designed by Arnolfo de Cambio, the Palazzo Vecchio was built in 1322 as the seat of the city's government, a function it still holds today. The original medieval interior was changed to suit the tastes of the Medici family in the 16th century and what you see inside today is largely their taste. The Salone de Cinquecento on the first floor was to be covered in frescoes by Leonardo da Vinci and Michelangelo, but Leonardo never quite worked out how to do frescoes and gave up, and Michelangelo got a better offer from the Pope, thus leaving us with the vastly inferior work of Vasari. Michelangelo's work is represented here though, with the *Victory*

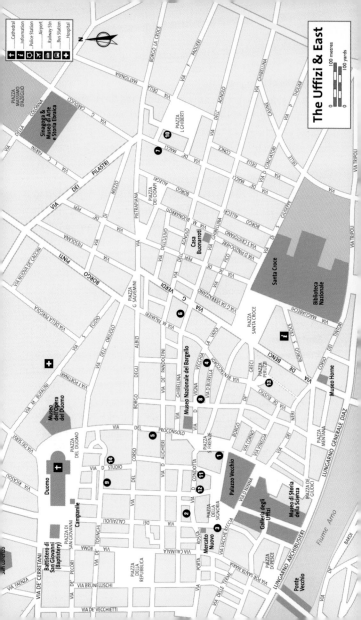

The Uffizi & East

Legend:
- Cathedral
- Information
- Police Station
- Airport
- Railway Stn
- Bus Station
- Hospital

0   100 metres
0   100 yards

Map Labels

- Sinagoga & Museo d'Arte e Storia Ebraica
- PIAZZA MASSIMO D'AZEGLIO
- PIAZZA L. GHIBERTI
- PIAZZA DEI CIOMPI
- Casa Buonarroti
- Santa Croce
- Biblioteca Nazionale
- PIAZZA G. SALVEMINI
- PIAZZA SANTA CROCE
- Museo Nazionale del Bargello
- Museo dell'Opera del Duomo
- PIAZZA DEL DUOMO
- Duomo
- Campanile
- Battistero di San Giovanni (Baptistery)
- PIAZZA DI SAN GIOVANNI
- PIAZZA DELLA REPUBBLICA
- PIAZZA DELLA SIGNORIA
- Mercato Nuovo
- Palazzo Vecchio
- Galleria degli Uffizi
- Museo di Storia della Scienza
- Museo Horne
- PIAZZA PERUZZI
- PIAZZA MENTANA
- PIAZZA GENERALE DIAZ
- PIAZZA DE' GIUDICI
- PIAZZA DI PESCIE
- Ponte Vecchio
- Fiume Arno
- San Lorenzo

statue. Next door peek into the Studiolo di Francesco I, decorated with frescoes of an alchemist's laboratory and the sciences. On the second floor in the Quartiere degli Elementi, Vasari has depicted the four elements, while the six rooms of the Quartiere de Eleonora – the apartments of Cosimo I's wife – are decorated by scenes of virtuous women. The Sala dei Gigli (room of the lilies) contains, among other things, Donatello's *Judith and Holofernes*. The bell tower beside the *palazzo* is the city's highest, at 94 m (308 ft), and contains the prison room where Savonarola (see page 62) saw out the last days of his life. Guided tours of the *palazzo* take you into rooms and passageways not accessible to the general public, last an hour and a half and are well worth the extra cost. English tours are popular and you should book in advance.

⊙ Piazza della Signoria **⊙** 055 2768224 **⊙** 09.00–19.00, closes at 14.00 Thur; admission charge

Santa Croce

A medieval survival, this originally simple church was built in 1228 by the newly established order of Franciscans. They were founded as an order that vowed poverty, but by the end of the century they were as rich and worldly as all the other religious orders and wanted to show off their wealth by building a flash new church. It was designed by Arnolfo di Cambio (who also designed the Duomo). The church is home to the tombs of a host of medieval and Renaissance names, including Michelangelo, Galileo, Ghiberti (who created the bronze doors of the Baptistery, see page 82), Machiavelli and others. The frescoes in the Bardi and Peruzzi chapels are by Giotto and depict the lives of St John the Baptist, St Francis and St John the Evangelist. In the Baroncelli chapel, the fresco by Gaddi is thought to be the first night scene ever depicted in a fresco.

Within the church is the entrance to Cappella dei Pazzi, a little domed chapel designed by Brunelleschi, which in turn leads into the cloisters, a haven from all the marble and artworks of the church. Across the courtyard is a little museum of church art, including some modern pieces by Pietro Parigi.

ⓐ Piazza Santa Croce ⓣ 055 246619 ⓘ 09.30–17.30 Mon–Sat, 13.00–17.30 Sun; admission charge

🔺 *Piazza della Signoria, where Michelangelo's* David *once stood*

Piazza della Signoria

The ancient parliament of the city, the square has grown in size
and impressiveness since its first incarnation as a forecourt to
the Palazzo Vecchio in 1307. The square became the place where
Florence's ruling families put on a show of wealth in the form of
statues of themselves and great works by then semi-famous
sculptors. Most of these have now been brought inside, out of the
weather, and replaced by replicas. Michelangelo's *David* originally
stood here (the original is now behind a protective barrier in the
Galleria dell'Accademia, see page 90). Other statues (or replicas) to
note are an equestrian statue of Cosimo 1, a seriously overwrought
fountain featuring Neptune by Ammannati, Donatello's *Judith and
Holofernes*, his *Marzocco* (the heraldic lion close to the Neptune
fountain), *Hercules and Cacus* by Bandinelli (on the steps opposite
the *Marzocco*), Cellini's bronze statue of Perseus holding the
Medusa's head, and the *Rape of the Sabine Women*, a tortuously
writhing piece carved out of a single block of flawed marble by
Giambologna in 1583. As you wander the square you might
cogitate on the day in 1497 when Savonarola lit his Bonfire of
the Vanities here – destroying what would now be a priceless
collection of art, aided and abetted by some of the men who
created them. A year later he stood tied to a stake in the exact
same spot, burning as a heretic.

Museo di Storia della Scienza

The 16th-century physicist, inventor and astronomer Galileo spent
some time in Florence, under the patronage of one of the Medicis
after he had been excommunicated by the Church. The museum
contains much of his equipment, including the lens he used to
identify the moon of Jupiter. It also, for some reason, contains one

of his finger bones, plus lots of beautifully made instruments and other good stuff. There are occasional demonstrations of some of the larger reconstructions of his experiments.

ⓐ Palazzo Vecchio ⓣ 055 2398876 ⓦ www.imss.fi.it ⓛ 09.30–17.00 Mon, Wed–Fri, 09.30–13.00 Tues, Sat, (summer); 09.30–17.00 Mon, Wed–Sat, 09.30–13.00 Tues (winter); admission charge

CULTURE

Casa Buonarroti

The house where Michelangelo never lived. His descendants lived here though and they collected memorabilia and a couple of good pieces – a bas relief Madonna and an unfinished *Battle of the Centaurs,* both the work of the artist in adolescence.

ⓐ Via Ghibellina 70 ⓣ 055 241752 ⓦ www.casabuonarroti.it ⓛ 09.30–14.00 Mon, Wed–Sun; admission charge

Galleria degli Uffizi

Really the Uffizi should be a whole area of the city all to itself. Set in a 16th-century palace built by Vasari for Cosimo I, it houses one of the finest art collections in the world. It is the personal art collection of several generations of the Medici family, the last of their line, Anna Maria Lodovica, bequeathing it to the state. There is no popping into the Uffizi – you book ahead and make the most of your visit or you queue along with the other 1,500,000 people who visit each year. Bring a floor plan with you and make sure you know what you want to see. Filippo Lippi and his pupil Botticelli are well represented, as are Michelangelo, Raphael, Titian, Leonardo, Mantegna, Caravaggio, Tiepolo, Rembrandt, Goya – it might be easier to list which of the world's artists aren't represented here

in profusion. Just steaming past the really famous stuff will take you about two hours. Get there early or book a tour with one of the many companies that will shepherd you past the best. For a break go out on to the Loggia de Lanzi terrace, where you are right under the campanile of the Palazzo Vecchio and can admire the clock face close up.

ⓐ Loggiatao degli Uffizi 6 ☎ 055 2388651 (info), 055 294883 (reservations line open 08.30–18.30 Mon–Sat)
ⓦ www.uffizi.firenze.it 🕒 08.15–18.50 Tues–Sun, until 22.00 in high summer; admission charge ❶ Pre-booking recommended

Museo Horne

The personal collection of Englishman Herbert Horne, this place is an eclectic mix of high art and domestic paraphernalia.
ⓐ Via dei Benci 6 ☎ 055 244661 🕒 09.00–13.00 Mon–Wed, Sat; admission charge

Museo Nazionale del Bargello

Named after the title of the 16th-century chief of police, this place has been a prison, a seat of government, a torture chamber and law courts, but in its current incarnation it holds the national collection of sculpture, most notably Michelangelo's *Bacchus Drunk*, Donatello's two sculptures of David and his St George.
ⓐ Via del Proconsolo 4 ☎ 055 2388606 ⓦ www.sbas.firenze.it/bargello 🕒 08.15–13.50 Tues–Sat (also 2nd & 4th Sun of the month & 1st, 3rd & 5th Mon of the month; admission charge

---

◀ *A copy of* David *stands outside the Palazzo Vecchio*

RETAIL THERAPY

Alessandro Bizzarri Bizzari by name and Bizzari by nature. Come here if you have a headache or other minor ailment for handmade herbal remedies. ⓐ Via Condotta 32r ① 055 211580 ⓛ 09.00–13.00, 15.30–19.00

Bortolucci The biggest collection of cutesy wooden clocks, Pinocchios, scooters and picture frames in the city. ⓐ Via Condotta 12r ① 055 211773 ⓦ www.bartolucci.com ⓛ 09.30–15.30, 18.15–23.15

Ethic A little work of art in itself, this sells interesting clothes and books, music and housewares too. ⓐ Borgo degli Albizi 37 ① 055 2344413 ⓦ www.ethic.it ⓛ 15.00–20.00 Mon & Sun, 10.00–20.00 Tues–Sat

Equoland Spend money and feel good at the same time. Lots of pretty ethnic jewellery and garments, and Fair Trade chocolate and coffee. ⓐ Via Ghibellina 115r ① 055 2645700 ⓦ www.equoland.it ⓛ 09.00–13.00, 15.30–19.30

Mercato di Sant'Ambrogio
Tasty picnic food in a smaller and less noisy version of Mercato Centrale. Outside are more domestic stalls – cheap underwear, some second-hand racks for fans of vintage clothes to rummage through, some crockery seconds worth browsing and more ⓐ Piazza L Ghiberti

Rosticceria
Spit-roast shop selling all manner of cooked and preserved goodies for a picnic, or for a little more you can eat in at the tables in the

back. Right across the road is their bar, All'antico Vinaio (65r) with two or three stools but lots of food from the *rosticceria* and a very Tuscan atmosphere. ➋ Via de Neri 74r ➊ 055 2382723 ➌ 08.00–21.00 Tues–Sat, 08.00–13.00 Sun

Via dei Calzaiuoli From Piazza Signoria to Piazza del Duomo, runs a broad pedestrianised road lined with tourist-oriented shops. At the south end is Coin at 56r, a department store with lots of good designs, clothes and accessories.

Wilma Right in the tourist heart of the city, so no big bargains in leather bags and shoes and more, but they do some wacky leather-covered crash helmets. ➋ Piazza San Firenze 16r ➊ 055 289087 ➌ www.wilmafirenze.it ➌ 10.00–19.30 Mon–Sat

TAKING A BREAK

Bar San Firenze £ ➊ Quiet *pasticceria* with lots of space, fabulous *gelati* and a solid collection of snacks and pizzas. ➋ Piazza San Firenze 1r ➊ 055 211426 ➌ 08.30–23.00

Caffè Italiano £ ➋ Stylish mahogany-lined café with tables for those with time to linger, or a bar for a quick espresso fix. Lunch specials are inexpensive. In a quiet side street; no outside tables. ➋ Via della Condotta 56r ➊ 055 291082 ➌ 08.30–20.30 Tues–Sun

Rivoire ££ ➌ The ultimate hang-out for people-watching in this fascinating square. Waiters in white jackets and bow ties, millions of pounds' worth of artwork to gaze at, excellent coffee and good hot chocolate. ➋ Piazza della Signoria 5r

t 055 214412 **w** www.rivoire.it **c** 08.00–24.00 Tues–Sun
i Closed two weeks in Jan

Vivoli ❹   A *gelaterie* with a big reputation in a side street close
to Santa Croce church. **a** Via Isola delle Stinche 7 (off via
Bentaccordi) **t** 055 292334 **w** www.vivoli.it **c** 07.30–24.00 Tues–Sat,
09.30–01.00 Sun **i** Closed during Aug

Yellow Bar ££ ❺   Brightly lit, noisy place serving great pasta and
pizzas, salads and more, plus you can watch the old lady actually
making the pasta while you wait. Street buskers wander in, people
queue all around you but the food is good and the clientele is as
much local office workers as tourists. **a** Via del Proconsolo 39r
t 055 211766 **c** 12.30–14.00

AFTER DARK

Restaurants

Boccanegra £–£££ ❻   Two shops, side by side. The main restaurant
is classy and innovative, with all the usual meat dishes but fish
dishes too and an excellent wine list, while next door is the
seriously unstuffy pizza section, bright and loud with pizza making.
a Via Ghibellina 124r **t** 055 2001098 (specify which restaurant
you're booking) **w** www.boccanegra.com **c** 19.00–24.00 Mon–Sat

Il Pizzaiuolo £–££ ❼   Neapolitan pizzas – the kind with the thicker
base – in this very popular place. Bare tables and walls, not
designed for a romantic night out – but good, well-made pizzas,

▶ *One of the joys of Italy are the* al fresco *meals*

plus lots of other options for anyone who doesn't want pizza and an opportunity to watch Florentines at dinner. ⓐ Via de' Macci 113r ⓣ 055 241171 ⓛ 12.30–15.00, 19.30–00.30

Aqua al Due ££ ⓼ Not a place for a romantic quiet evening but has a good vibe and lots of bustle. ⓐ Via dell'Aqua 2r ⓣ 055 284170 ⓛ 18.00–23.00

Coquinarius ££ ⓽ Possibly the best value in this part of the city. Traditional Tuscan food – hare sauce, octopus carpaccio, pear and cheese ravioli. Good for vegetarians as well as carnivores. ⓐ Via delle Oche 15r (off Via de Tosinghi) ⓣ 055 2302153 ⓛ 12.00–23.00, 23.30 Fri & Sat ⓘ Closed three weeks in Aug

Caffè Cibrèo £££ ⓾ Huge reputation among locals but also draws in the tourists. The dessert menu is excellent. Advisable to book. ⓐ Via Andrea del Verrocio 5r (off Piazza L Ghiberti) ⓣ 055 2345853 ⓛ 08.00–01.00 Tues–Sat

Frescobaldi £££ ⓫ A warren of deep red, grey and umber rooms link this classy restaurant and wine bar. Spend the evening over a meal as close to innovative as Florence gets or snack on *aperitivo*, tapas or cheese plates in the wine bar. Vegetarians will do well here. ⓐ Via dei Magazzini 2–4r (off Via Condotla) ⓣ 055 284724 ⓦ www.frescobaldi.it ⓛ 12.00–14.30, 19.00–22.30 Tues–Sat, Mon dinner only

Gustavino £££ ⓬ Modern steel and glass in this wine-oriented restaurant. Open kitchen and smart service. ⓐ Via della Condotta 37r ⓣ 055 2399806 ⓦ www.gustovino.it ⓛ 19.30–23.00

Osvaldo £££ ⑬   Blink and you'd miss this place – no outside tables, a tiny sign on the door but a good reputation with local people. Try goose with truffles for a special treat. Good fish options but vegetarians might struggle. ❷ Piazza Peruzzi 3r ❶ 055 217919 ❷ 19.00–22.30 Mon–Sat

Ristorante I Caminetto £££ ⑭   Aimed at the tourist trade with menus in English and a very attractive seating area outside. In a quiet square behind the Duomo, this is a place for a posh night out. Simple dishes are cooked well and if the garden seating doesn't appeal, the interior is just as attractively laid out. ❷ Via dello Studio 34r ❶ 055 2396274 ❿ www.ristorante-ilcaminetto.it ❷ 19.00–23.00 Thur–Tues

Bars & clubs
Loggi del Grano Caffè Café with large tourist-oriented menu but pretty outside tables and a cool young feeling inside. Nightly music in the bar upstairs. ❷ Piazza del Grano ❶ 055 295422 ❷ 07.30–24.00

I Visacci This deeply cool wine bar will appeal to the young and arty. Bright colours, Latin American music every night, aperitifs from 18.30 and good food. ❷ Borgo Albizi 80r ❶ 055 2001956 ❷ 10.00–22.00 Mon–Wed, 10.00–02.00 Thur–Sat, 15.30–21.00 Sun

Blob Club Happy hour between 18.00 and 21.00 and a very young crowd. Free admission. ❷ Via Vinegia 21r ❷ 18.00–03.00

Jazz Club Long-established basement club with live music most nights. ❷ Via Nuova de'Caccini 3 ❶ 055 2479700 ❷ 21.00–02.00 Mon–Fri, later Sat, closed July & Aug

Piazza della Repubblica & Around

This is the part of the city which you are most likely to encounter in your first few minutes in Florence. The train and bus station can be a scary place for new arrivals but the taxi rank at the front of the station will get you to your hotel and the tourist office inside the station provides help, accommodation and maps. This part of the city is dominated by the two piazzas, Repubblica and Santa Maria Novella. The chief attraction here is shopping, with all the big designer names and lots of small boutiques filled with clothes, housewares and, most of all, shoes!

SIGHTS & ATTRACTIONS

Piazza Santa Trinità

Surrounded by *palazzos* and centred by a granite pillar from the Roman baths at Caracalla, the piazza is a busy thoroughfare. At its south is the Ponte Santa Trinità, its stonework originally placed there in 1567 and then replaced in 1944 after the retreating German army scattered them. Legend has it that Michelangelo designed the bridge and from its centre there are fine views of the surrounding hills, of the Palazzo Corsini's statues against the skyline and of the Ponte Vecchio.

Mercato Nuovo

Mercato Nuovo means new market – that is 'new' in the sense of 16th-century. A market has been here since the 11th century; and the current new loggia is a mere 400 years old. As with the Little Mermaid in Copenhagen and the Leaning Tower in Pisa, so in Florence you have to have your photo taken here in the market

Piazza della Repubblica & Around

0   200 metres
0   200 yards

N

Cathedral
Information
Police Station
Airport
Railway Stn
Bus Station
Hospital

VIA LA PIRA
Università
PIAZZA DELLA
SS. ANNUNZIATA
Opificio delle
Pietro Dure
PIAZZA S
CROCE
VIA DEL
ORIUOLO
Corte
d'Assise
Museo
San Marco
PIAZZA SAN
MARCO
Galleria
dell'Accademia
VIA DEGLI ALFANI
VIA DEI SERVI
VIA M. BUFALINI
Museo
dell'Opera
del Duomo
BORGO DEGLI ALBIZI
VIA GHIBELLINA
Museo del
Bargello
PIAZZA S
CROCE
VIA SAN GALLO
DELLE RUOTE
VIA XXVII APRILE
VIA SAN ZANOBI
VIA CAVOUR
VIA GUELFA
VIA DE PUCCI
VIA RICASOLI
Duomo
PIAZZA DEL
DUOMO
VIA DELL'ORIUOLO
VIA DEL PROCONSOLO
BORGO DE CERCHI
Palazzo
Vecchio
Museo di Storia
della Scienza
VIA NAZIONALE
VIA XXVII APRILE
PIAZZA
INDIPENDENZA
VIA C. BATTISTI
VIA CAVOUR
VIA DE GINORI
Palazzo Medici
Riccardi
VIA DE' GORI
PIAZZA DI
MERCATO
CENTRALE
VIA PANICALE
VIA NAZIONALE
VIA FAENZA
San Lorenzo
VIA DE CERRETANI
Campanile
Battistero di
San Giovanni
VIA DE PECORI
VIA ROMA
PIAZZA DELLA
SIGNORIA
PIAZZA DELLA
REPUBBLICA
Mercato
Nuovo
Galleria
degli Uffizi
V. CALIMALA
VIA DE CALZAIUOLI
VIA PANZANI
VIA FIUME
Palazzo dei
Congressi
VIALE FILIPPO STROZZI
VIA VALFONDA
PIAZZA
DELL'UNITÀ
ITALIANA
PIAZZA
DELLA
STAZIONE
Santa Maria
Novella
S M Novella
VIA DE BANCHI
VIA DELLA SCALA
VIA DELLA SCALA
VIA DEL SOLE
VIA DE TORNABUONI
Palazzo
Strozzi
V DEGLI STROZZI
VIA DELLA VIGNA NUOVA
VIA PORTA ROSSA
BORGO SS APOSTOLI
PIAZZA S.
TRINITÀ
Santa
Trinità
Ponte
Vecchio
LUNGARNO ACCIAIUOLI
LUNGARNO CORSINI
PONTE
S TRINITÀ
V. DE' RONDINELLI
Via dei Fossi
VIA DELLA SCALA
VIA PALAZZUOLO
Ognissanti
BORGO OGNISSANTI
PIAZZA
OGNISSANTI
V. M. FINIGUERRA
V. DELLA SPADA
VIALE FRATELLI ROSSELLI
VIALE BELFIORE
Giardino
Corsini
IL PRATO
PIAZZALE
DI PORTA
AL PRATO
VIA DELLA SCALA
VIA IL PRATO
VIA MAGENTA
VIA SOLFERINO
PIAZZA C
GODDINI
Fiume Arno
PONTE
ALLA
CARRAIA
PIAZZA DEL
CARMINE
Santa Maria
del Carmine
BORGO SAN FREDIANO
LUNGARNO SODERINI
PONTE A
VESPUCCI
PIAZZA DI
CESTELLO
VIA DE SERRAGLI
BORGO S JACOPO
Santo
Spirito
VIALE FRATELLI ROSSELLI
VIA JACOPO DA DIACCETO
VIA L ALAMANNI
Stazione di
Porta al Prato
VIA DEL PONTE ALLE MOSSE
PIAZZA
VITTORIO
VENETO
LUNGARNO AMERIGO VESPUCCI
VIA MONTE BELLO
VIA MAGENTA
VIA DELLA FONDERIA
PONTE
DELLA
VITTORIA
VIA PISANA
PIAZZA T
GADDI
PIAZZA P
VETTORI
VIALE ARIOSTO
VIA DEL ORTO
VIA G CARELLI
V ALEARDO ALEARDI
Fiume Arno
VIALE LINCOLN

with *Il Porcellino*. The bronze fountain dates from the 17th century and its original, a Roman marble, is in the Uffizi. The market is full of tourist goodies and in the evening it is a pleasant place to watch the buskers.

ⓐ Via Por Santa Maria ⓛ 09.00–19.00 Apr–Oct; 09.00–19.00 Tues–Sat, Nov–Mar

Ognissanti

The Church of All Saints was the family church of the explorer Amerigo Vespucci who gave his name to the new landmass that Columbus had discovered. The new continent and the young Amerigo are portrayed in the *Madonna della Misericordia* by Ghirlandaio inside the church. Also here is Botticelli's fresco *St Augustine*. Botticelli is buried here. In the adjoining refectory is Ghirlandaio's *Last Supper*. Visit early in the morning when the monks are gliding about to the sound of choral music.

ⓐ Borgo Ognissanti 42 ⓣ 055 2398700 ⓛ 07.30–12.30, 15.30–19.30

Ponte Vecchio

The Arno has been spanned by a bridge at this point since the Romans first settled here in 59 BC. This one dates back to the 14th century and was one of the few bridges to escape destruction by the retreating German army in World War II. The goldsmiths and jewellers have been here since 1593. Before that the bridge was the home of tanners and butchers, a slightly less romantic proposition than today. The bridge is lined on both sides by shops, some of which have extensions hanging over the water. You will notice lots of padlocks locked on to iron rings set in the walls of the bridge. Lovers fix the padlocks and throw the key into the river as a sign of their enduring love. A corridor called the Vasari corridor links the Palazzo Vecchio on the north side with the Palazzo Pitti on the south, and was built to allow the Medici to travel from one of their palaces to the other without coming in contact with the riff raff. During the daytime the bridge is a lively place. The shops offer everything from junk earrings to classy antiques, but there are few bargains. Just enjoy the atmosphere of it all.

Santa Trinità
Originally a simple 11th-century church, this place became more ornate as the centuries passed and the monastic order which built it adjusted their vows of poverty to their increasing wealth. The interesting features are Ghirlandaio's 15th-century frescoes, which actually portray local figures of the time – the Medici's bank manager, Francesco Sassetti and his wife who put up some of the cash, Ghirlandaio himself (the first dark-haired shepherd in the Nativity scene), Lorenzo de Medici and various family members. In one scene St Francis is portrayed in Piazza Santa Trinità so you can see what it looked like in the 15th century.
ⓐ Piazza Santa Trinità ☎ 055 216912 ⏰ 08.00–12.00, 16.00–18.00 Mon–Sat, 16.00–18.00 Sun

CULTURE

Museo di Santa Maria Novella
The old cloisters of the monastery of Santa Maria Novella have been converted into a museum. On display here are the frescoes in the Spanish chapel used by the Spanish family members of Cosimo I's wife. They depict more salvation and damnation, this time featuring the Dominicans themselves as the hounds of the

Lord (Domini canes – a play on the name Dominican), saving souls and punishing those who will not be saved. The frescoes are by Andrea di Firenze.

ⓐ Piazza Santa Maria Novella ☏ 055 282187 🕐 09.00–17.00 Mon–Thur, Sat, 09.00–13.00 Sun; admission charge

Santa Maria Novella

This former monastery came into existence in the 13th century, built by the Dominicans, a particularly fundamentalist group who actively sought out heretics to burn and torture. The exterior was given a 15th-century facelift and extension, paid for by a family of merchants called Rucellai, whose name modestly appears on the upper storey that they paid for. Inside, note the way that the length of the church is given an apparent extension by building the columns closer and lower as they approach the altar. What draws the visitor into this church, though, are its decorations: frescoes by Masaccio that must have astonished the 15th-century congregation with their innovative sense of depth and perspective; Giotto's Crucifix of 1288; and Filippo Lippi's 15th-century cycle of frescoes in the little chapel to the right of the chancel. Around the altar, Ghirlandaio has created a series of frescoes of scenes from the New Testament that say more about 15th-century life than they do about the birth of the Virgin Mary or John the Baptist. If you haven't used up all your fresco appreciation by now, look in the Cappella Strozzi at the end of the left transept, which contains frescoes by Nardi di Cione that are probably his masterpiece. The people who shelled out for the painting are shown being led into heaven by St Michael while those who missed out on

◀ *Florence's famous bronze boar,* Il Porcellino

(or couldn't pay for) penance are seen being shovelled into hell.
Life was simpler then.

ⓐ Piazza Santa Maria Novella ❶ 055 215918 ⓛ 09.30–17.00
Mon–Thur, 13.00–17.00 Fri & Sun; admission charge

RETAIL THERAPY

This part of the city is where the serious shoppers come. Via de
Tornabuoni is designer heaven with all the big names (Ferragamo
(14r), Enrico Coveri (81r), Emilio Pucci (20r), Armani (48–50), Gucci
(73r), Prada (67r), Versace (13–15), Bulgari (61r), Parenti (67r) – you
get the drift) lined up, each with one or two amazingly expensive
items in their windows. For less well-known, but almost affordable
boutiques, Via della Vigna Nuova, Via Porta Rossa and Via Roma
are full of tiny shops. Ponte Vecchio is the home of jewellers.
The following are a tiny sample – serious shoppers should get
out and enjoy.

Emilio Cavallini Tiny shop with t-shirts, underwear, matching tights
and tops and socks, all in original prints. ⓐ Via della Vigna Nuova 24r
❶ 055 2382789 ⓦ www.emiliocavallini.com ⓛ 10.00–19.00 Mon–Sat,
1500–19.00 Sun

Eredi Chiarini Very Italian men's clothes, classic and elegant.
ⓐ Via Roma 16r ❶ 055 2844781 ⓦ www.eredichiarini.com
ⓛ 09.30–19.30 Tues–Sat, 15.30–19.30 Mon

Farmacia Santa Maria Novella The poshest soap ever, in an ancient
pharmacy. ⓐ Via delle Scala 16 ❶ 055 216276 ⓦ www.smnovella.it
ⓛ 09.30–19.30 Mon–Sat

Forno Top Good bakery close to the station. Lovely cakes, focaccia, sandwiches. ⓐ Via delle Spada 23r, (off Via del Sole) ⓣ 055 212461 ⓛ 07.30–13.30, 17.00–19.30 Mon–Sat, closes early Wed

Furla Beautiful bags, shoes, watches and belts in respectable plain leather or crazy patterns. ⓐ Via della Vigna Nuova 47r ⓣ 055 282779 ⓦ www.furla.com ⓛ 10.00–19.30 Mon–Sat, 11.30–19.30 Sun

Liu Jo Very cool place, with several branches in the city. From delicate frocks to combats, jewellery and boots to match. ⓐ Via della Vigna Nuova 28r ⓣ 055 2654692 ⓦ www.liujo.it ⓛ 10.00–19.30 Tues–Sat, 11.30–13.30, 14.30–19.00 Sun, 15.30–19.30 Mon

Margherita Conad One of a chain of small supermarkets around the city. ⓐ Via L Alamanni 2–10r ⓣ 055 211544 ⓛ 08.00–19.30 Mon–Sat

Mercato Nuovo Home of the recently padlocked bronze boar, whose nose you must rub if you wish to return to the city, this place sells plastic Davids, Duomos, aprons with bits of anatomy printed on, bags, belts, scarves, junk jewellery – all the things you need to take home for your relatives. ⓐ Off Via Calimala ⓛ 09.00–19.00 Mon–Sat

Mui Mui For those who can't afford Prada, here are their young, cheaper clothes. ⓐ Via Roma 8r ⓣ 055 2608931 ⓦ www.muimui.com ⓛ 10.00–19.00

Raspini Vintage If you can't afford the Armani or Prada in the Raspini shop in Via Roma, come here for last year's stuff at almost

affordable prices. ⓐ Via Calimaruzza 17r ☎ 055 213901
ⓦ www.raspinivintage.it 🕐 10.30–19.30 Tues–Sat, 15.30–19.30
Sun & Mon

Rinascente Lovely department store in the old-fashioned sense,
with designer concessions, lingerie, beautiful linens and a rooftop
café with views. ⓐ Piazza della Repubblica 1 ☎ 055 219113
ⓦ www.rinascente.it 🕐 09.00–21.00 Mon–Sat, 10.30–20.00 Sun

TAKING A BREAK

Piazza della Repubblica is the place to people-watch and there
are some good cafés to do it in. Along Via delle Spada are several
good places to buy picnic food – try Franco Moreno at 46r
(🕐 08.00–13.00, 17.00–19.30), while almost opposite is Panifico,
a bakery (07.45–13.00, 17.00–19.30).

Caffè Gilli ££ ❶ Occupying pride of place in Piazza delle Repubblica
is this Florence institution, gloriously decorated inside but with a
large garden of potted plants in the square, protecting its streetside
customers from view while affording them the opportunity to study
passers by. ☎ 055 213896

AFTER DARK

Funiculi £ ❷ Enormous pizza place, with four groaning pizza
ovens, some lovely vegetarian options, all ingredients from Naples,
and some other dishes if you are all pizza'd out. Not for a romantic
dinner for two. ⓐ Via Il Prato 81r ☎ 055 2646553 🕐 12.00–15.00,
19.00–01.00 Mon–Fri, evenings only Sat & Sun

Il Contadino £ ❸   Equally well suited for an inexpensive lunch if you are in the area, this no-nonsense place offers set meals at eye-wideningly inexpensive prices. Very popular with the backpacking crowd. ⓐ Via Palazzuolo 71r ⓛ 11.00–15.00, 19.00–24.00, closed Sun (& Sat in July & Aug)

Officina Move Bar £ ❹   This very cool place has a chameleon quality to it – in the mornings it's a grab-a-pastry breakfast bar, while at lunch it's a good, inexpensive café with a changing daily menu of pizzas, pastas and salads. At night it reinvents itself as a disco bar with aperitifs with your cocktails at 19.30, followed by any and all kinds of music, occasionally live. ⓐ Via il Prato 58r Santa Maria Novella ⓣ 055 210399 ⓛ 08.00–02.00 Mon–Fri, 18.30–03.00 Sat & Sun
ⓘ Closed August

Rosticceria della Spada ££ ❺   Really a traditional Tuscan takeaway place, this shop now has tables in a plain, unfussy dining room where you can eat the food. It has a good inexpensive set menu for lunch and dinner, and the à la carte is also affordable. Takeout costs about half as much. ⓐ Via delle Spade 62r (off Viadel Sole) ⓣ 055 218757 ⓦ www.laspadaitalia.com ⓛ 12.00–15.00, 18.00–22.30

Osteria dei Cento Poveri £££ ❻   In a quiet backstreet behind Santa Maria Novella, this little gem of a restaurant offers lots of fish options on the menu – sea bass, sea bream or lobster gnocchi. ⓦ Via Palazzuolo 31r ⓣ 055 218846 ⓛ 12.30–14.30, 19.00–24.00 Wed–Sun, closed Tues for lunch

The Duomo & North

The area to the north of the city centre is home to some seriously big guns in the tourist itinerary. The Duomo is really the centre of the city – all roads seem to lead you there and all views include a little bit of the Duomo. North of it is the Accademia, which you will identify as you approach from the queues of people waiting to get in. North again is San Marco, one of the finest small museums in the city. San Lorenzo is another big draw, as is its museum with statuary by Michelangelo inside. The market stalls around San Lorenzo and the Mercato Centrale are also good. In all there are many days' worth of sightseeing to do here.

SIGHTS & ATTRACTIONS

Baptistery

This tiny octagonal church, dedicated to St John the Baptist, was built in the 11th century. Highlights of the church include amazing mosaics decorating the domed ceiling, representing the Last Judgement and the mouth of hell. The doors of the church are also fascinating. Cast in bronze, the doors depict the life of John the Baptist (south doors, 1330s, Andrea Pisano), the story of Christ (north entrance, commissioned 1401, Lorenzo Ghiberti) and stories from the Old Testament (east doors 1424–52, Lorenzo Ghiberti). The east doors are clearly the finest but the originals are safely stowed away in the Museo dell'Opera del Duomo. People who know about that stuff consider these panels to be the first indication of the yet to occur Renaissance with their focus on lifelike figures and sense of perspective. Incidentally you can see Ghiberti in the bronze door frame – the fourth head down on the right-hand side.

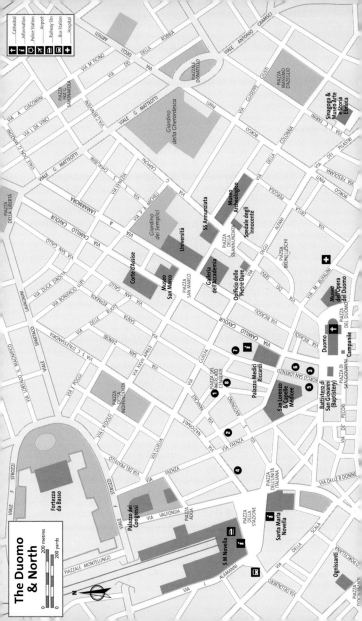

The Duomo & North

Legend:
- ✚ Cathedral
- ⓘ Information
- Police Station
- ✈ Airport
- 🚇 Railway Stn
- 🚌 Bus Station
- ✚ Hospital

Scale:
- 0 — 200 metres
- 0 — 200 yards

Labelled places:

- VIA A GIACOMINI
- PIAZZA FRA G. SAVONAROLA
- VIALE DON G. MINZONI
- VIA M FICINO
- VIA DELLA ROBBIA
- VIA ARTISTI
- VIA ANTONIO
- VIALE ANTONIO GRAMSCI
- PIAZZETTO DONATELLO
- PIAZZA MASSIMO D'AZEGLIO
- VIA GIUSEPPE GIUSTI
- VIALE G. MATTEOTTI
- Giardino della Gherardesca
- VIA GINO CAPPONI
- VIA GIUSEPPE
- PIAZZA DELLA LIBERTÀ
- VIALE G. MATTEOTTI
- Sinagoga & Museo Arte e Storia Ebraica
- VIA FARINI
- VIA PILASTRI
- VIA LAMARMORA
- VIA CAVOUR
- VIA SAN GALLO
- VIA VENEZIA
- VIA MICHELI
- VIA P.A. MICHELI
- Giardino dei Semplici
- Università
- SS Annunziata
- Museo Archeologico
- PIAZZA DELLA SS.ANNUNZIATA
- Spedale degli Innocente
- VIA DELLA COLONNA
- BORGO PINTI
- VIA DELLA PERGOLA
- VIA FIESOLANA
- BORGO
- Corte d'Assise
- Museo San Marco
- PIAZZA SAN MARCO
- Galleria dell'Accademia
- Opificio delle Pietre Dure
- PIAZZA BRUNELLESCHI
- ✚ (Hospital symbol)
- Museo dell'Opera del Duomo
- VIA M. BUFALINI
- VIA DUCA D'AOSTA
- VIA BONIFACIO LUPI
- VIA SANTA REPARATA
- VIA DELLE RUOTE
- VIA XXVII APRILE
- VIA ZANOBI
- VIA RICASOLI
- VIA CAVOUR
- VIA CAMILLO
- ⓘ ❼
- PIAZZA DEL DUOMO
- Duomo
- Campanile
- VIA RICASOLI
- Battistero di San Giovanni (Baptistery)
- PIAZZA DI SAN GIOVANNI
- VIA DE' PECORI
- ❽ PIAZZA DEL MERCATO CENTRALE
- ❶
- Palazzo Medici Riccardi
- BORGO SAN LORENZO
- ❻
- San Lorenzo & Capelle Medicee
- ❺
- VIA DE' GINORI
- VIA DE' CERRETANI
- VIA DELL'ARIENTO
- VIA FAENZA
- ❷
- VIA NAZIONALE
- VIA GUELFA
- VIA S. C. D'ALESSANDRIA
- VIA DELLE RUOTE
- VIA S. ZANOBI
- VIALE F. STROZZI
- VIALE SPARTACO LAVAGNINI
- VIALE LAVAGNINI
- VIA F. POGGI
- VIA S. CATERINA D'ALESSANDRIA
- PIAZZA INDIPENDENZA
- VIA XXVII APRILE
- VIA G. LA PIRA
- VIA REPARATA
- VIA DELLE
- Fortezza da Basso
- VIALE FILIPPO STROZZI
- Palazzo dei Congressi
- VIA VALFONDA
- PIAZZA ADUA
- ❹
- VIA FAENZA
- PIAZZA DELL'UNITÀ ITALIANA
- PIAZZA DELLA STAZIONE
- ⓘ
- 🚇
- VIA NAZIONALE
- VIALE FILIPPO STROZZI
- PIAZZALE MONTELUNGO
- ⓘ S M Novella
- 🚇
- Santa Maria Novella
- VIA DELLA SCALA
- VIA L. ALAMANNI
- VIA VALFONDA
- VIA DELLE BELLE DONNE
- VIA DEL MORO
- VIA DELLA SCALA
- Ognissanti
- VIA PALAZZUOLO
- PIAZZA S M Novella

🅐 Piazza San Giovanni 🕐 12.00–19.00 Mon–Sat, 08.30–14.00 Sun; admission charge

Duomo

Size, it seems, matters. The Duomo dominates the Florentine skyline and 600 years since it was begun, it is still the biggest masonry dome in the world. The cathedral is actually called Santa Maria del Fiore. Built mostly between 1296 and 1436 when the dome was completed, but still being embellished in 1887, it puts the fuss over Wembley Stadium in perspective. You can just hear Brunelleschi, the engineer of the dome, telling Piero de Medici 'I'll have it finished by Saturday guv'.

Four generations of architects lived out their lives building the cathedral. The real sight is the exterior, with three colours of marble inlaid in patterns. Only the south side is really old – the rest is a 19th-century reconstruction. The interior is positively austere, compared to the flashy outside. The inside of the dome contains frescoes of hell and the Last Judgement, painstakingly painted on to the wet plaster by Vasari and Federico Zucchari, who painted likenesses of many of the city's movers and shakers into his work. You could also check out the crypt which contains the remains of Santa Reparata, the 4th-century church that stood here before the Duomo, some Roman remains and the tomb of Brunelleschi, the man who finally got the roof on.

The dome itself, accessed from outside the cathedral, can be climbed for adjective-defying views of the city. It's a stiff climb, not for the claustrophobic or faint of heart.

Beside the cathedral its 14th-century bell tower, the Campanile, was built by an assortment of famous names – Giotto, Pisano and Francesco Talenti. This last, less well-known architect was responsible for thickening the walls at the base of the Campanile, thus avoiding another leaning tower coming into existence. A climb to the top is less scary than climbing the Duomo, and gives nice views over the city and of the Dome itself.

Santa Maria del Fiore ⓐ Piazza del Duomo ☏ 055 2302885
🕙 10.00–17.00 Mon–Wed, Fri (until 15.30 Thur, until 16.45 Sat), 13.30–16.45 Sun

Dome 🕙 08.30–19.00 Mon–Fri, 08.30–17.40 Sat, closes at 16.00 first Sat of month); admission charge

Santa Reparata 🕙 10.00–17.00 Mon–Wed, Fri (until 15.30 Thur, until 16.45 Sat), 13.30–16.45 Sun; admission charge

Campanile 🕙 08.30–19.30; admission charge

> ### BUILDING THE BIGGEST DOME IN THE WORLD
> In medieval times, domes were built using a technique developed by the Romans – creating a wooden shell and building around it. The shell supported the bricks until it was complete and the bricks could hold themselves in place. This dome was to be so big that no wooden structure could support it until it was stable. The problem was solved by building two shells of stone beams and filling each with a herringbone pattern of bricks.
>
> Construction took 16 years and the workers stayed up in the dome all day, eating their lunch where they worked to save the 40 minutes trekking up and down each lunchtime.

Giardino dei Semplici
The Dominican nuns who once owned this 2-ha (5-acre) plot must have seriously irritated Cosimo I, because he seized their land and

created a physic garden here – Pisa and Padua had one so the Medicis had to have one too. The garden grew medicinal herbs, as it still does, but now it has become the city's botanic gardens and tropical plants have been added to the herbs. At the entrance to the garden is Museo di Geologia e Paleontologia, full of bones and fossils which make a nice change from all the displays of elaborate gorgeousness in the other museums and churches.

ⓐ Via Micheli 3 ❶ 055 2757402 ● 09.00–13.00 Mon–Fri, closed Mon in summer months; admission charge

Museo di Geologia ● 09.00–13.00 Wed, Fri, June–Sept; 09.00–13.00, 14.00–17.00 Tues, 14.00–17.00 Wed–Sat, Oct–May

Palazzo Medici Riccardi

Currently government offices but once yet another palace owned by the Medici, this is partly open to the public and is worth a visit for the Gozzoli frescoes, supposedly representing the journey of the Magi but in reality glorifying the Medici name by depicting them as the three kings. Individual Medicis can be made out in the frescoes, notably Lorenzo the Magnificent on a grey horse apart from the rest of the procession. On the first floor of the building is a Madonna and Child by Filippo Lippi and in the gallery there is more Medici bombast in the ceiling fresco, representing the ascent to heaven of the entire Medici family. As you enter the building, admire the windows on either side of the entrance – designed by Michelangelo.

ⓐ Via Camillo Cavour 1 ❶ 055 2760340 ● 09.00–19.00 Thur–Tues; admission charge ❶ Book ahead in high summer or if there is an exhibition

◀ *The Duomo*

San Lorenzo

This ancient church designed by Brunelleschi and paid for by the
godfather of the Medici clan, Giovanni di Bicci de' Medici, was
clearly never completed, as the bare bricks on the façade indicate.
Giovanni ran out of cash, his son Cosimo put up some more to
complete the interior but plans for the exterior never saw fruition,
despite the fact that Michelangelo himself drew them up. There
is much to look out for in the church. The bronze pulpits and doors
of the Old Sacristy are by Donatello, while Filippo Lippi painted an
annunciation in the north transept. On the north wall of the
church is a tortured *Martyrdom of St Lawrence* by Bronzino.
Generations of the Medici are buried in the side chapels of this
church. Cosimo's tomb, in the centre of the church, is labelled
Pater Patriae (Father of the Fatherland) – no modesty here. More
Medici are in the Sagrestia Vecchia. Giovanni is here with two of his
grandsons, amid beautiful decorations by Donatello.

You have to shell out again if you want to see the rest of the
Medici funerary ornaments, made by Michelangelo himself.
The Cappelle Medicee is entered from Piazza Madonna degli
Aldobrandini. Past the Medici minions in the crypt, and the later
royal Medicis in the Chapel of the Princes, you come to the
Sagrestia Nuova and the three tombs designed and carved
(two of them at least) by Michelangelo. He portrays the two
Medici men with contrasting characters: the one, Lorenzo, Duke
of Urbino as a philosopher, the other, Giuliano, Duke of Nemours as
an action man. Opposite them is the uncompleted *Madonna and
Child*, finished off by Michelangelo's assistants. Next door to the
church is the Biblioteca Medicea-Laurenziana, designed by Leonardo
to hold the Medici collection of important papers and books. The
vestibule is open to the public, although the reading room itself

may not be. The staircase, in a style now called Mannerist, has
wavy steps flowing down into the room while the walls are
decorated with disappearing columns that hold nothing up,
and empty niches.

Church 🅐 Piazza San Lorenzo 🕻 055 216634 🕘 10.00–17.00 Mon–Sat;
admission charge.

Cappelle 🕘 08.30–17.00 Tue–Sat, 08.30–13.50 Sun, closed Mon.

Biblioteca 🕘 08.30–13.30 Mon–Sat; free

Santissima Annunziata

Another church, this one with a painting by an angel, rather than of
an angel, built in its current format in the 15th century. The portico
contains frescoes by Andrea del Sarto and others, damaged in the
flood of 1966. Inside is the painting begun in 1252 by one of the monks
and finished off by an angel while he slept. Traditionally Florentine
newlyweds come here to lay a bouquet by the Virgin to ask for a
fruitful marriage. Above the entrance porch to the cloister of the dead
(full of memorial tablets) is del Sarto's *La Madonna del Sacco*.

🅐 Piazza della Santissima Annunziata 🕻 055 266181 🕘 07.30–12.30,
16.00–18.30

Spedale degli Innocente

The first orphanage in Europe, this building, designed by
Brunelleschi and opened in 1419, was commissioned by the silk
weavers' guild and took in foundlings that were placed on the
rotating stone at the left of the loggia. Entrance to the cloisters
inside is free. The museum upstairs contains a little cache of
Renaissance art including an adoration of the Magi by Domenico
Ghirlandaio. Outside check out the piazza with its two wacky
Mannerist fountains by Pietro Tacca. If you are in Florence on

25 March, the Feast of the Annunciation, come here to see
the fair.

ⓐ Piazza della Santissima Annunziata 12 ❶ 055 2491708
🕐 08.30–14.00 Mon, Tues, Thur–Sun; admission charge
for museum

CULTURE

Galleria dell'Accademia

Some people say the reason they come to Florence at all is to visit
the Accademia, the home to Michelangelo's statue of David.
It's a good idea to have visited the Bargello first to see other
representations of the image of the youth who killed the powerful
warrior and then come to see this. The figure stood for hundreds
of years out in the open in Piazza della Signoria but is now safely
wrapped up in here. There's a good gadget beside it which lets you
manipulate representations of bits of it for a closer look. The *David*
isn't the only reason to come here though. The other statues by
Michelangelo, all unfinished (you will notice while you are here that
the great man had no problem with having to see a job through to
the end) are almost as fascinating, since you can see the work in
progress (he always left the hands until last!).

ⓐ Via Ricasoli 58–60 ❶ 055 2388609 🕐 08.15–18.50 Tues–Sun;
admission charge

Museo Archeologico

In all this surfeit of Renaissance and medieval art it is easy to forget
that Florence was Roman, and before that Etruscan. This museum

---

▶ *To see Michelangelo's* David *is some people's sole reason for visiting Florence*

remedies the omission with displays of Etruscan and Roman art. There are also exhibits of Egyptian and Greek artefacts.

ⓐ Via della Colonna 38 ❶ 055 23575 ⓦ www.commune.fi.it/sogetti/sat ❶ 14.00–19.00 Mon, 08.30–19.00 Tues & Thur, 08.30–14.00 Wed, Fri, Sun; admission charge

Museo dell'Opera del Duomo

The museum is filled with beautiful things but the high point is Michelangelo's *Pietà*, carved in the artist's old age and intended for his tomb. In his rage at the unsatisfactory nature of his work the artist smashed Christ's leg but the sculpture was repaired by his assistants. In the upper floors look out for life-sized figures carved by Donatello.

ⓐ Piazza del Duomo 9 ❶ 055 2302885 ⓦ www.operaduomo.firenzi.it ❶ 10.00–18.00 Mon, Wed–Sun; admission charge

Opificio delle Pietre Dure

A museum depicting the work of mosaic making. The museum not only has exhibits of tools and methods, but actually restores ancient mosaics.

ⓐ Via degli Alfani 78 ❶ 055 218709 ❶ 08.15–14.00 Mon, Wed, Fri, Sat, 08.15–19.00 Thur; admission charge ❶ Make an appointment to watch the restoration work

San Marco

The former convent of the Dominican order of San Marco is now a museum, largely dedicated to the work of Fra Angelico, a brother and later the prior of the convent. In the downstairs rooms are works by Fra Angelico, Ghirlandaio and others, many of them repeated, showing the way that artists churned out paintings to order – these were not carefully thought out masterpieces but factory-made stuff. The portrait of Savonarola, who lived here for a time and whose rooms upstairs contain fragments of his clothes and possessions by Fra Bartolomeo, depicts him as a seriously fundamentalist figure. The cells upstairs are the biggest reason to visit here. Painted by Fra Angelico and his assistants, each room contains a little sacred fresco. Towards the end they must have run out of ideas since the images begin to repeat themselves. At the top of the stairs is one of the most breathtaking paintings in Florence – Angelico's *Annunciation*.

ⓐ Piazza San Marco 1 ❶ 055 2388608 ❷ 08.15–13.50, Tues–Fri plus 1st, 3rd, 5th Mon of month, 08.15–19.00 2nd & 4th Sun of month; admission charge

Sinagoga & Museo di Arte e Storia Ebraica

An elaborate 19th-century synagogue, with a museum telling the history of the Jews in Florence. ⓐ Via Farini 4 ❶ 055 2346654 ❷ 10.00–17.00 Sun–Thur, Apr–Sept; 10.00–15.00 Sun–Thur, 10.00–14.00 Fri, Nov–Mar; admission charge

RETAIL THERAPY

Borgo San Lorenzo This street, which runs north from Piazza di San Giovanni, is filled with some good cafés and small boutiques with inexpensive clothes to admire. Check out Dixie at 5r, Zini at 26r, Trench at 10r and Romaro Firenze at 3r with some very cute shoes. Lots of handbag shops, plus some old familiars – Benetton, Footlocker et al.

Collections Alice Atelier The strangest commedia dell'arte masks you ever saw – leaf masks, daisy masks, Pinocchio masks, wooden puppets, carvings and more. ⓐ Via Faenza 72r ⓣ 055 287370 ⓛ 09.00–13.00, 15.30–19.30 Mon–Sat

⬤ *Shopping in delicatessens can result in delicious picnics*

Il Papiro Classic paper products shop with beautiful hand-bound notebooks, Christmas cards which will impress your friends and lots of other handmade goodies. ⓐ Piazza del Duomo 24r ☎ 055 281628 🕐 10.00–13.00, 14.00–19.00

Johnsons & Relatives One of the better paper products shops – boxes, lampshades, writing paper and lots more. ⓐ Via Camillo Cavour 49r ☎ 055 2658103 🕐 10.00–13.00, 14.00–19.00 Mon–Sat, 10.00–18.00 Sun

Mercato Centrale The biggest fresh food market in the city, this one is good for picnic food, watching Florentines at work and for the many souvenir and clothes stalls around the square. The market is usually a mornings-only affair, but one or two of the restaurants serving market workers are open all night. ⓐ Piazza del Mercato Centrale 🕐 07.00–14.00 Mon–Sat, 16.00–20.00 Sat in winter

San Lorenzo Market Hundreds of stalls surround San Lorenzo church. You can stock up on gifts to take home for the family, add to your handbag collection with a good fake or splash out on a leather coat. 🕐 09.00–19.00

TAKING A BREAK

Alberto Buonocare £ ❶ Pretty pizza place dominated by a gigantic pizza oven. Traditional pizzas. ⓐ Piazza del Mercato Centrale 22r ☎ 055 211131 🕐 11.00–24.00

Antica Pasticceria Sieni £ ❷ Glorious pastry shop with wonderful things made of chocolate, lovely cakes and, for sensible people, pasta and salads too. ⓐ Via de Aviento 27r (off Via Panicale) ⓒ 08.00–19.00, Tues–Sun

La Cantinietta £ ❸ Like Nannini across the road, only louder, brasher and more of it. Bruschetta, pasta, pizzas, lovely desserts. ⓐ Borgo San Lorenzo 12r ⓒ 11.30–22.00

La Lampara £ ❹ Brush past the naff-looking menu in assorted languages in the window, pass the stacked up logs for the pizza oven, ignore the indoor tables and head out to the pretty courtyard garden. Good inexpensive food, traditional dishes, popular with locals. ⓐ Via Nazionale 36r ⓣ 055 215164 ⓒ 12.00–23.30

Nannini £ ❺ Big caff-style place with cakes to make you drool, more substantial pastas and rolls waiting in hot trays and a bar for slurping espresso or a glass of wine. Table service costs more than standing at the bar which costs more than a takeout. ⓐ Borgo San Lorenzo 7r ⓒ 07.30–20.00

Nuti ££ ❻ Pasta and pizza dishes. Two shops, one a *pizzeria* and the other a *trattoria*. Seriously popular and fills out at lunch and dinner. ⓐ Borgo San Lorenzo 22–24r ⓣ 055 210145 ⓒ 11.30–01.00

AFTER DARK

Restaurants
Caracol £ ❼ Fed up with pizza and pasta? Come to this Mexican café bar for some familiar fajitas, quesadillas, enchiladas and

guacamole, followed by a very happy hour from 18.00–20.00.
Live music on Fridays. ⓐ Via Ginori 10r ⓣ 055 211427 ⓛ 17.30–02.00
Tues–Sun, closed Mon

Trattoria Zà Zà ££ ⓫   The classiest of the many restaurants around
the Central Market. Inside is all stone walls and Chianti bottles but
outside is the nicest with a large area of the square sectioned off.
Set menus in the evening can be less expensive. ⓐ Piazza del
Mercato Centrale

Pubs & clubs

Astor Café This about as unFlorentine as bars get. The Astor is loud,
shiny and new. Good food during the day, *aperitivo* at 19.00,
followed by cocktails and jazz downstairs. ⓐ Piazza del Duomo 20r
ⓣ 055 284306 ⓛ 12.30–03.00

BZF Great food, Internet café, bookshop, nice bar and live jazz. ⓐ Via
Panicale 61r ⓣ 055 2741009 ⓦ www.bzf.it ⓛ 16.00–24.00 Tues–Sun,
closes June–Aug

Maracana Casa di Samba A little like the Ilford Palais on a Saturday
night in the 1960s, except with nearly naked women. Brazilian
cabaret dancers in a huge ballroom with a balcony and dance floor.
Nice lobby. ⓐ Via Faenza 4 ⓣ 055 210298 ⓛ 12.00–04.00 Tues–Sun;
admission charge ⓘ Closed June–Aug

The Fish Pub Blasting the night away with all sorts of offers on beer
and shots at this 'Scottish' pub. Happy hour from 16.00–20.00. Pick
up a flyer for a free drink or be female on a Monday for free drinks
all night. ⓐ Piazza del Mercato Centrale 44r

Oltrarno

Oltrarno is the place to come when the tour groups have finally got you down. It's not that there are no tourists here, but that there is so much more space they seem less oppressive. There's a rural feel to this side of the city, with the huge Bóboli Gardens and quieter, greener piazzas. If the little artisan shops are giving way to elegant restaurants and expensive shops there are still lots of sights to see. Over to the west is the church of Santo Spirito, a must-see for its frescoes, while Palazzo Pitti will astound you with the wealth of the people who built it and you can bask in the work of Raphael and Titian. To the east is Piazzale Michelangelo, crowded but stunning. Set off as dusk falls and be at the Piazzale for sunset and evening. Amazing.

SIGHTS & ATTRACTIONS

Giardino di Bóboli

Laid out in High Renaissance style in 1550, when the Medici family had bought up the palace that Luca Pitti had gone into negative equity with. The gardens were originally a sandstone quarry, but were developed into ornate gardens, with clipped box hedges, an artificial lake and island, wild areas of cypress and ilex trees and various follies. They were once full of high maintenance art – Michelangelo's *Quattro Prigioni* (now in the Accademia) were once here, as was Giambologna's *Oceanus* (now in the Bargello). Many originals are still here including the classical statues that line Vittolone, the cypress avenue. The gardens get packed out in summer but if you want to get away from the crowds wander down to the southwest corner. Don't miss: the amphitheatre,

built out of the quarry, La Grotta Grande and L'Isolotto, the
artificial island.

a Piazza dei Pitti **t** 055 2651838 **c** 08.15–19.30, closes earlier in
winter; admission charge

Museo Bardini

Architectural salvage is all the rage in modern cities these days,
but Stefano Bardini had the good sense to carry out a bit of his own
in the 19th century, when all kinds of medieval and Renaissance
buildings were being demolished to make way for Piazza della
Repubblica. Palazzo Bardini, built in 1883, is mostly salvaged
medieval and Renaissance stonework and carpentry. It's one of
the nicer museums of the city – no big names decorate the walls
but the place is full of stuff Bardini bought up when no one realised
what it was all going to be worth in a few years.

a Piazza de'Mozzi 1 **t** 055 2342427 **i** The museum was closed
for restoration in 2006 so check to see if it is reopened.
Admission charge

Museo degli Argenti

This place gives some indication of just how fabulously wealthy the
Medici must have been. Not only did they build all those palaces
and churches and collect all that art, they also had the wherewithal
to store up this little treasure house. Ivory, silver, gold, jewellery,
Roman glassware, amber, inlaid ebony furniture, and portraits of
the family.

a Piazza dei Pitti **t** 055 2388709 **c** 08.15–16.30 Oct–Mar (until 18.30
Apr, May, Sept, until 19.30 June–Aug), closed 1st & last Mon of
month; admission charge

Museo La Specola

More a sight than a cultural institution this museum, deep in the university buildings, makes a serious change from frescoes and statuary, although Leonardo would surely have approved. It's a kind of natural history museum filled with shells and bugs and stuffed animals. The Cere Anatomiche has the weirdest waxworks you ever saw. They were created as teaching aids in the 18th century and consist of lots of wax models of dissected bodies, each displaying a separate set of muscles, arteries and other internal bits and pieces. If that isn't graphic enough, there is a tableaux representing the horrors of the plague.

@ Via Romana 17 ☏ 055 2288251 ☉ 09.00–13.00 Mon, Tues, Thur–Sat; admission charge ❶ Bring your camera – photography is allowed

Palazzo Pitti

Once the main residence of the magnificent Medici family, this place just grew and grew. For a while, when Florence was briefly the capital of Italy, it was the home of the Italian royals but now it is a complex of museums, the best of which is the Galleria Palatina (see page 104). Also in here are the Royal apartments, a sumptuous spread of 18th–19th century magnificence – ornate ceilings, enormous four poster beds and paintings of the Medici. The Parrot Room is covered in beautiful silk cloth, detailed with bird designs. Also worth a visit are the Gallerie del Costume, the carriage museum, the Museo degli Argenti (opposite) and the Galleria d'Arte Moderna (page 104).

@ Piazza dei Pitti ☏ 055 2388614 ☉ 08.15–18.50 Tues–Sun; admission charge

Piazzale Michelangelo

A stirring walk up from the river, the Piazzale Michelangelo is usually packed to the gills with tour buses but the views are truly worth the trek and bus-dodging.

San Miniato al Monte

Offering even more stirring views than in Piazzale Michelangelo below, the 13th-century façade of San Miniato al Monte is covered in green and white inlaid marble. Legend tells that a church was built here after Saint Miniatus was decapitated in AD 250 down by the river, then picked up his head and climbed the hill to this spot. The nave has more inlaid marble, there are lovely old frescoes on the walls and an 11th-century barrel vaulted crypt. Photographs are allowed and entrance is free. Surrounding the church are its burial grounds, the grand mausoleums stacked one above the other.
ⓐ Via delle Porte Sante 34 ⓣ 055 2342731 ⓛ 08.00–19.30 (summer); 08.00–12.00, 14.30–18.00 (winter)

Santo Spirito

Set in the disarmingly parochial Piazza Santo Spirito, this church has been called the most beautiful church in the world (by Bernini – perhaps he didn't get out much) and was designed for the most part by Brunelleschi. The exterior was never finished but was planned to follow the unusual outlines of the 38 chapels surrounding the central nave. Besides admiring the elaborate architecture of the interior look out for Filippino Lippi's *Madonna and Child* in the Nerli Chapel.
ⓐ Piazza Santo Spirito ⓣ 055 210030 ⓛ 10.00–12.00, 16.00–17.30 Mon–Fri, 16.00–17.30 Sat & Sun

Via Maggio

When the Medici moved out to Oltrarno, they made this side of the river a pretty desirable area and there followed a spree of *palazzo* building during the 15th and 16th centuries. The *palazzos* are not open to the public as sights but many of them are antique shops where you can pretend to be buyers and admire the interiors.

◯ *It's a bit of a trek to Piazzale Michelangelo, but the view is worth the effort*

CULTURE

Cenacolo di Santo Spirito

Santo Spirito once had a monastery attached. All that survives today is its refectory, now a museum displaying a collection of 11th-century Romanesque sculpture. Better than this though, and worth the charge, is the beautiful pre-Renaissance *Crucifixion* (1360–65), attributed to the school of Andrea Orcagna.

ⓐ Piazza Santo Spirito ☎ 055 287043 ⏰ 09.00–14.00 Tues–Sun (summer); 10.30–13.30 Tues–Sun (winter); admission charge

Galleria d'Arte Moderna

This gallery of modern art is only modern in relation to the age of everything else in museums in Florence. Paintings from as early as 1784 are here, and there is little after 1945. They are mostly the art collection of the Dukes of Lorraine, who lived in the palace for a while. There are about 30 rooms of paintings but the really interesting stuff is the work of the 19th century *Macchiaioli* (spot makers), the Italian version of the Impressionists.

ⓐ Piazza dei Pitti ☎ 055 2388601 ⏰ 08.15–13.50 Tues–Sat (open some Mon & Sun); admission charge

Galleria Palatina

If Florence had only this one art gallery you'd still think it was worth the flight. The arrangement of the paintings in here is not structured as you would expect in an art gallery. They are in the places chosen for them by the Grand Dukes, and chronological order was not a requirement. The rooms themselves are like little art galleries, painted with ceiling frescoes by Pietro da Cortona. Other rooms include a suite built for Napoleon after his conquest of northern Italy in 1813. The real draw to the Galleria Palatina, however, is the collection of more than 1,000 paintings. There are paintings here by Botticelli, Andrea del Sarto, Tintoretto, Caravaggio, Rubens and Van Dyck. Several works by Titian are here, including his *Mary Magdalene* and *La Bella*, a portrait of an unknown woman. Raphael's *Madonna of the Chair* is here, as is *Donna Velata*, a portrait of Raphael's mistress, a baker's daughter.

ⓐ Piazza dei Pitti ⓣ 055 2388614 ⓛ 08.15–18.50 Tues–Sun; admission charge

Santa Felicità

Possibly the oldest church in town, but seriously remodelled by Brunelleschi in the 1420s and Vasari in 1565 to accommodate the Vasari corridor (the passageway the Medici used when walking from one palace to another, to avoid coming into contact with the common people). Besides admiring the church, look out for two works by Mannerist artist Pontorno, the *Annunciation* and the *Deposition*.

ⓐ Piazza di Santa Felicità ⓣ 055 213018 ⓛ 09.00–12.00, 15.00–18.00 Mon–Sat

Santa Maria del Carmine

A major stop on the culture vulture trail, this church is famous for the Brancacci Chapel. The frescoes here are a perfect illustration of how chance events can have an enormous effect. The chapel's frescoes were commissioned by Felice Brancacci, who paid the painter Masolino (1383–1447) to do the work. Two years into the work, Masolino took off for Hungary, where he had more work to do and left his young assistant to keep things going until he got back. The result was a series of frescoes of the life of St Peter by Masaccio

(1401–28), whose work surpassed his master's and set a standard
for generations of Renaissance artists to follow. Masaccio didn't
live to complete the work, which Filippino Lippi took on in 1480.
Get here early, it's worth it.

ⓐ Piazza del Carmine ⓣ 055 2382195 ⓛ 10.00–17.00 Mon, Wed–Sat,
13.00–17.00 Sun; admission charge

RETAIL THERAPY

There are little shops tucked away all around western Oltrarno, but
the big street for shopping is Via Guicciardini. Leather shoes, bags
and clothing line the street and you should look out for Giotto
Leather at 22r, GABS at 130 and Mannina at 16r.

Casini Accessible and affordable pretty clothes, shoes and bags. If
you don't like the clothes check out the art on the walls. ⓐ Piazza dei
Pitti 32–33r ⓣ 055 2608730 ⓦ www.jtcasini.com ⓛ 10.00–19.00
Mon–Sat, 11.00–18.00 Sun

Emporium Lots of well-designed and clever household things –
an umbrella in a box, spoons for getting olives out of the jar,
crazy clocks – things you never knew you needed until now.
ⓐ Via Guicciardini 122r ⓣ 055 212646 ⓛ 10.00–19.00 Mon–Sat,
11.00–17.00 Sun

Giotto Leather Lovely shoes, coats and bags. ⓐ Via Guicciardini 22r
ⓣ 055 287741 ⓛ 10.00–19.00 Mon–Sat, 11.00–19.00 Sun

Giuditta Blandini Attractive clothes made from natural fibres
and dyes. No sandals and caftans here – some very stylish clothes.

📍 Via dello Sprone 25r 📞 055 2776275 🌐 www.stilebiologico.it
🕐 09.30–13.00, 15.30–19.00

Giullio Gianni e Figlio Award-winning store-made leather bound
and marbled paper, books, cards and more. 📍 Piazza dei Pitti 36r
📞 055 212621 🕐 10.00–19.30 Mon–Sat, 10.30–18.30 Sun

🔺 *There's no shortage of stalls selling leather goods*

Madova Tiny shop selling gloves made in its on-site factory.
🅐 Via Guicciardini 1r 🆃 055 2396526 🅛 09.30–19.00 Mon–Sat

TAKING A BREAK

Cabiria Café £ ❶ Tables out in the piazza in front of Santo Spirito church or inside this inexpensive café bar, popular with tourists. Menus in English, children's menu, huge breakfast menu. Salads, bruschetta, and more substantial dishes. 🅐 Piazza Santo Spirito 4r
🆃 055 215732 🅛 09.00–24.00 Wed–Mon

Caffè I Ricchi £ ❷ A quiet spot in Piazza Santo Spirito, this café offers good lunch options and a great *gelaterie*. 🅐 Piazza Santo Spirito 9r 🆃 055 215864 🆆 www.caffericchi.it 🅛 07.00–01.00 (summer); 07.00–20.00 (winter)

Caffè Pitti £–££ ❸ Good set lunch options at this café bar, with seating inside the pretty café or tables outside in the relatively quiet street. Pannini and other snacks also available. Nice views of the Palazzo Pitti. Open until late with an à la carte dinner menu and jazz at weekends. 🅐 Piazza dei Pitti 9 🆃 055 2399863 🅛 10.00–24.00 Tues–Sun

AFTER DARK

Restaurants
BorgoAntico £–££ ❹ One of an increasing crowd of good cafés and restaurants in Piazza Santo Spirito, this one offers a slew of pizzas, a set lunch menu and reasonably priced dishes from the menu. Usually good, fresh seafood options. 🅐 Piazza Santo Spirito 6r
🆃 055 210437 🅛 12.00–13.30, 19.00–23.30

Il Santo Bevitore £–££ ❺ This wine bar with a good food menu has the look of a monastery refectory about it. Popular for an inexpensive lunch of salads, soup, pasta and some interesting main courses, and a good quiet drinking spot in the evening. ⓐ Via Santo Spirito 64–66r ❶ 055 211264 ⓦ www.ilsantobevitore.it ❶ 12.30–14.30, 19.30–23.30 Mon–Sat, 19.30–23.30 Sun

Trattoria 4 Leone ££ ❻ This place comes into its own in the summer when the tables out in the square fill up with a lively young crowd. Tuscan cuisine. ⓐ Piazza della Passera ❶ 055 218562 ❶ 12.00–14.30, 19.00–23.00, evenings only Wed

Beccofino ££–£££ ❼ If you wondered where all the innovative cooking went on in Florence, this is a good example of it. Modern cooking based on Tuscan recipes and a good wine selection from the attached wine bar. Reservations recommended and expect it to get noisy when the place is full. Riverbank terrace in the summer is a little more peaceful. ⓐ Piazza degli Scarlatti 1r ❶ 055 290076 ⓦ www.beccofino.com ❶ 19.00–23.30 Tues–Sun

Osteria Santo Spirito ££–£££ ❽ The best of the places to eat in Piazza Santa Spirito, this one serves Tuscan food with some interesting twists to it. Tables inside the modern dining room or in summer out in the piazza. ⓐ Piazza Santa Spirito 16r ❶ 055 2382383 ❶ 12.00–14.30, 19.30–23.30

Onice £££ ❾ A treat for a special occasion, this Michelin-star place in the exclusive Villa la Vedetta Hotel offers an artful menu of Italian dishes, influenced by the chef's sojourn in Thailand. Pink silk banquettes and alligator skin tables and overwhelming service add to the sense of being truly pampered. In summer, eat out on the terrace with all of Florence spread before you. A six-course Menù Degustazione or choosing from the à la carte isn't cheap, but it's certainly an experience. ⓐ Viale Michelangelo 78 ⓣ 055 681631 ⓛ 19.30–23.00

Bars & Clubs

Caffè la Torre Live music most nights in an attractive riverside café. ⓐ Lungarno Cellini 65r ⓣ 055 680643 ⓦ www.caffelatorre.it ⓛ 10.30–03.00

Dolce Vita If you wondered where all the cool people are in Florence, it's here among the pink vinyl cushions and gold and umber bar. Pop in for the aperitifs around 19.00 and stay for cocktails, music and mood. ⓐ Piazza del Carmine ⓣ 055 284595 ⓦ www.dolcevitaflorence.com ⓛ 19.00–02.00 Tues–Sat

James Joyce This place comes into its own in summer when the big, enclosed garden offers a cool place to enjoy the lively atmosphere. Happy hour 19.30–21.30 with free *aperitivo*. ⓐ Lungarno Benvenuto Cellini 1r ⓣ 055 6580856 ⓛ 18.00–02.00 Tues–Thur, until 03.00 Fri–Sun

⊙ *The soft colours of Siena and its Duomo*

OUT OF TOWN
trips

Pisa

With the advent of budget airlines, Pisa is fast becoming a major hub in the tourist industry, a position it hasn't held since the 13th century when the Arno began to silt up, disconnecting the city from its lucrative maritime trade. In the intervening centuries Pisa has quietly slumbered away, its medieval buildings intact and its tower leaning a little more each year until underpinning work began in 1989. Academic institutions make the city a very young place with a lively nightlife, there is the huge attraction of the Campo dei Miracoli, some serene public gardens, a few shops to check out and some good cafés. The tourist office (📞 050 560464 🕐 09.00–18.00 Mon–Sat, 10.30–18.30 Sun) is in Piazza del Duomo, next door to the ticket office for the sights of the Campo dei Miracoli. There is another good tourist office at the airport (📞 050 503700). Pisa is best accessed from Florence by the Terravision bus from Piazza delle Stazione. Departure times are listed in front of the departure point and a ticket seller waits at the departure point to sell tickets. Reserve a seat at weekends. 🌐 www.lowcostcoach.com

There is also a regular train service from Florence to Pisa, which is cheap to use.

SIGHTS & ATTRACTIONS

Campo dei Miracoli

This is the place that everyone knows about without ever knowing how, one of the most photographed places in the world. The lawns where the leaning tower, the Duomo and the Baptistery are all located make a little sight in themselves. Come here on a busy day

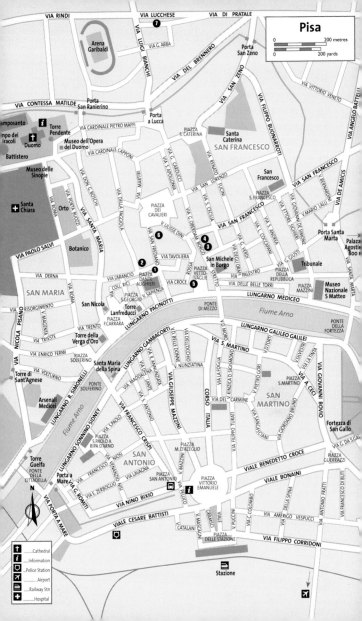

and watch people queuing up to pretend they are holding up the tower while their friends take their photo, or stroll past the stalls selling all manner of leaning tower memorabilia – tea towels, t-shirts, plastic models, chocolate, umbrellas – the list is endless.

Baptistery (Battistero)

Older than the church buildings at the heart of Florence, this Baptistery dates back to Pisa's time as the leading mercantile light during the 12th century, although the domed roof is a later 14th-century addition. Inside, the major attraction is the 1260 pulpit, designed by Nicola Pisano and carved with scenes from the life of Christ.

ⓐ Campo dei Miracoli ❶ 050 560547 ⓦ www.opapisa.it
🕓 09.00–20.00 Apr–Sept, 09.00–18.00 Mar, Oct, 09.00–17.00 Nov–Feb; admission charge

Camposanto

The cemetery where the important Pisans were buried is lined by a cloistered wall which had a series of 14th-century frescoes by Benzozzo Gozzoli, until an Allied plane bombed them in 1944. The few which survived depict, appropriately enough, visions of hell and death.
🕓 09.00–18.00 Apr–Sept, 09.00–17.00 Mar & Oct, 08.30–19.30 Nov–Feb; admission charge

Duomo

This place, begun in 1063, makes Florence's Duomo a mere stripling (in age if not in size). The outside of the building is by far the most impressive part. The façade is 12th century and inlaid with glass, majolica and sandstone knots, flowers and animals. Lower down is plain white marble. High up in the west façade is the tomb of Buscheto, the architect of the building. A lot of the interior was damaged by a fire in 1595. Paintings and the pulpit, lost in the fire, were replaced thanks to Medici money. At the east side is the Portale San Ranieri with bronze doors (1180) by Bonnano Pisano. Here, as in the rest of the exterior, there are Arabic influences in the designs in the bronze and the patterns in the inlaid façade.

ⓐ Campo dei Miracoli ❶ 050 560547 Ⓦ www.opapisa.it
🕑 10.00–20.00 Mon–Sat, 13.00–20.00 Sun, Mar–Sept, 10.00–13.00, 15.00–17.00 Mon–Sat, 13.00–17.00 Sun, Oct–Mar; admission charge

Leaning Tower (Torre Pendente)

If you ignore the fact that the tower you are looking at is seriously leaning over and just look at it as a piece of architecture it is actually quite beautiful. It is eight storeys high and hollow at its core (otherwise it would have fallen over centuries ago). Inside, a spiral staircase works its way up to the belfry with its seven bells at the top. Six of the storeys consist of colonnaded galleries, with doors leading from the staircase out onto them. On the ground floor a frieze indicates that the tower was begun in 1173. ❶ To climb the tower you must book online, or at the booking office in person in advance, at least 15 days before you plan to visit. The climb is pricey but worth it. Anyone under 18 must be accompanied by an adult.

ⓐ Campo dei Miracoli Ⓦ www.opapisa.it

Orto Botanico

A pleasant spot for a picnic, this is the oldest botanic garden in Europe.

ⓐ Via L Ghini 5 ❶ 050 551345 🕑 08.00–17.00 Mon–Fri, 08.00–13.00 Sat

A LUCRATIVE ERROR

A bit of a disaster from the start, the tower took 200 years or so to build (1173–1350) and was leaning by 1274 when the fourth storey was added. By 1350 it was 1.4 m (5 ft) off kilter and it continued to slide a little more each year for six centuries until, by 1993, it was 5.4 m (18 ft) askew. The tower was built on sand, which accounts for its problems. Work began in 1989 to correct the lean, although for a time things got slightly worse. Underpinning has corrected the lean by about 40 cm (16 in) and the tower is considered safe once more, although they let only 30 people in at a time. Who would have guessed when it started to lean that the tower would generate so much interest purely by virtue of its faults!

Piazza dei Cavalieri

This is the heart of the student quarter of Pisa, a wide open square surrounded by *palazzos*. On the north side is the Palazzo dei Cavalieri, designed by Vasari as the headquarters of the Cavalieri de San Stefano, an order of knights created by Cosimo I. Covered in white designs marked on to the plaster, it is currently the home of the Scuola Normale Superiore, a college of Pisa University. Before this 16th-century building went up, the medieval town hall stood here. All but the council chamber, which still survives as a lecture theatre, was demolished on the order of Cosimo I, when the city came under Medici rule. The man on the horse in the square is Cosimo himself. Beside it is the knights'

▶ *The Leaning Tower peeping round the Duomo*

> **A FATHER'S REVENGE**
> Opposite the Palazzo dei Cavalieri is the Palazzo dell'Orologico, incorporating the medieval jail where in 1288 Count Ugolino, the mayor, accused of treachery was walled up along with his sons and grandsons whom, the story goes, he proceeded to eat in order to stay alive. In Dante's *Inferno* Count Ugolino is condemned to hell where he feeds forever on the head of Archbishop Ruggieri, the man who pointed the finger at him.

church, the Chiesa dei Cavalieri, whose walls are hung with the battle standards of the knights.

San Nicola
This tiny 11th-century church dedicated to Pisa's patron saint contains a painting showing Pisa during the plague. Its campanile also leans.
ⓐ Via Santa Maria 2 ☎ 050 24677 🕒 08.00–12.00, 17.00–18.30

San Paolo Ripa d'Arno
If you are passing it is worth checking out this 12th-century church built in the same style as the Duomo. It has an impressive façade while inside is a chapel dedicated to St Agatha and built, unusually, entirely of brick, even its cone-shaped roof.
ⓐ Piazza San Paolo a Ripa d'Arno ☎ 050 41515 🕒 Open only by arrangement

Santa Maria della Spina
This tiny bright white Gothic church is a notable feature of the riverscape. It isn't named after the many spiny rills and flutes of its

exterior, but after one of the thorns from the crown of thorns on Christ's head which was kept here for a time. History doesn't say what happened to it.

ⓐ Lungarno Gambacorti ❶ 050 32154 🕒 10.00–14.00 Tues–Sun, longer hours in summer

CULTURE

Museo dell'Opera del Duomo

The building was once the chapter house of the cathedral and now holds monuments from the piazza brought in out of the weather and from the Duomo and Baptistery, considered too fragile to remain in situ. It offers an opportunity to see much of the exquisite inlay work close at hand and, for once, there are good displays explaining the exhibits. Look for the hippogriff looted during the wars against the Saracens. There are also collections of Roman and Etruscan remains and from the cloister, good views of the tower.

ⓐ Piazza Duomo ❶ 050 560547 🕒 08.00–19.30 Apr–Oct, 09.00–17.30 Nov–Feb; admission charge

Museo delle Sinopie

When the war was over and people began to pick up the pieces in the Camposanto they discovered that, although the frescoes had disintegrated, the outlines that the artists had drawn underneath in the original layer of plaster were intact. These have been reconstructed and brought together in this museum and, like the unfinished Michelangelo statues in Florence, give a fascinating insight to the technicalities of the work of the artists. In addition to these originals, the museum gives a good account of how frescoes are put together. Well worth visiting before you go to Florence.

ⓐ Piazza del Duomo ⓑ 08.00–19.30 Apr–Sept, 09.00–17.30 Mar &
Oct, 09.00–16.30 Nov–Feb; admission charge

Museo Nazionale di San Matteo

Once the medieval convent of San Matteo, this attractive
Gothic building now houses the slightly disorganised Pisan art
collection. While the medieval stuff is worth seeing, particularly
Nino Pisano's *Madonna del Latte*, the real gems are the Renaissance
paintings. There are works here by Masaccio, Donatello, Fra
Angelico and Ghirlandaio.
ⓐ Piazza San Matteo in Soarta ⓣ 050 541865 ⓑ 08.30–19.00,
until 13.00 Sun; admission charge

RETAIL THERAPY

The two main shopping streets in town are Borgo Stretto and Corso
Italia, and although neither of them come up to the standards of
gorgeousness of Siena or Florence, there are a few good places to
check out.

Corso Italia is the more respectable shopping street. Its small
shops, still family-run businesses, now vie for space with the usual
suspects – Max Mara, Footlocker and Benetton. At the head of the
street is an arcaded market selling second-hand books. Look out for
Di Banchi at number 3, selling some classy clothes and shoes while
next door is another very traditional shoe shop

Borgo Stretto is more avante-garde, lined with interesting
boutiques as well as a small market of things aimed at the tourist
market. Adjoining the street is Vettovaglie market, where *cavolo*

◀ *The immense Baptistery at Pisa*

nero and globe artichokes are in great profusion, alongside aubergines and peppers. Around the market are some interesting shops. Nepal Tibet Jewellery has artefacts and jewellery from the East, while Delicatessen Cesqui (ⓐ Number 38 ☎ 050 580269 🕒 07.00–13.30, 16.00–20.00) is a great place to pick up supplies for a picnic. Right next door is an excellent bakery.

TAKING A BREAK

Caffeteria Dantesca £ ❶ The best of several café bars in this quiet, green square, this place offers lots that could make a substantial lunch, from pizzas to pasta and filled rolls. *Gelaterie* and cakes too. ⓐ Piazza Dante Alighieri ☎ 050 46280 🕒 06.30–21.00

Café Pasticceria Macchi £ ❷ Set in the quiet Piazza Dante Alighieri, this café bar serves lots of tasty snacks and more substantial dishes, along with the usual wine and espresso at the bar. Tables outside under an awning make this a great place for a stop. ⓐ Via Tanucci 7 ☎ 050 56100 🕒 06.30–19.00

Lo Spisio £ ❸ Tables under the loggia of the building as well as inside this place is good for a pit stop, as well as more substantial meals. ⓐ Borgo Stretto 56 ☎ 050 580082 🕒 08.30–21.00

Salza £–££ ❹ Pretty tables under the loggia of the building, lovely cakes and sweets as well as a full restaurant menu. ⓐ Borgo Stretto 56 ☎ 050 580144 🕒 07.45–20.30

▶ *A mouthwatering gelato is always a good idea*

AFTER DARK

Restaurants

La Mescita ££ ❺ In a quiet corner of Piazza Vettovaglie, this place serves traditional Tuscan food with a twist. A place for a special occasion. ⓐ Via Cavalca 2 ❶ 050 544294 ⓦ www.lamescita.it 🕐 12.30–14.30, 20.00–22.30 Tues–Fri, 13.00–20.00 Sat & Sun ❶ Closed three weeks in Aug

Osteria dei Cavalieri ££ ❻ Popular with students and staff from the university, this inexpensive place is set in a medieval tower house. Lunch specials are particularly good value but the evening menu can offer some excellent traditional Tuscan food without damaging your wallet too badly. ⓐ Via San Frediano 16 ❶ 050 580858 🕐 12.30–14.00, 19.30–22.00 Mon–Fri, evenings only Sat

Aphrodite £££ ❼ A little way out of the centre of town, this place is worth seeking out for its modern design and creative cooking, especially if you have tired of the usual Tuscan menus. In summer, eat out in the cool of the garden. ⓐ Via Luchesse 33A ❶ 050 830248 ⓦ www.ristoranteaphrodite.com 🕐 18.00–01.00 Tues–Sun

Clubs & bars

Borderline Occasional live music in this laid-back place, focusing on blues and country. ⓐ Via Vernaccini 7 ❶ 050 58077 ⓦ www.borderlineclub.it 🕐 21.00–02.00 Mon–Sat; admission charge for live music nights

Dottorjazz Jazz club with lots of mood close to the railway station.
🅐 Via Vespucci 10 🕿 339 8619298 🕒 21.00–02.00 Tues–Sat,
closed June–Sept; admission charge

ACCOMMODATION

Albergo Galileo £ B&B, centrally located, with original frescoes on
the walls. Only nine rooms. 🅐 Via Santa Maria 12 🕿 050 40621

Campeggio Villaggio Internazionale £ 🕿 050 500470
🅔 campstm@iol.it Campsite with good facilities located at
the Marina di Pisa at the coast and accessible by CPT bus from
Piazza Sant'Antonio 🕿 050 505511

Hotel Roseto £ One of the best bargains in Pisa, this 2-star hotel
has big airy rooms, a pretty garden, a roof terrace with lovely views
and is centrally located. 🅐 Via Mascagani 24 🕿 050 42596
🆆 www.hotelroseto.it

Hotel Repubblica Marinara ££ All mod cons in this purpose-built
small hotel, about 1 km (½ mile) from the town centre. Internet
access, great breakfast (no cappuccino and croissant at this place)
and a courtesy bus to anywhere in town. 🅐 Via Matteucci 81
🕿 050 3870100 🆆 www.hotelrepubblicamarinara.it

Royal Victoria ££ A hotel with a long history, catering to tourists for
over 100 years. Rooms are full of antiques, nice roof terrace, very
central, views over the river, lots of charm. 🅐 Lungarno Pacinotti 12
🕿 050 940111 🆆 www.royalvictoria.it

OUT OF TOWN

Siena

Siena is accessible from Florence by bus, which depart every
30 minutes from the SITA bus station in Via St Caterina da Siena.
Journey time is an hour and a quarter. Be careful to take the Corse
Rapide bus or you will visit several towns en route. Trains also make
the journey from Santa Maria Novella Station, but usually involve
changing trains at Empoli and a journey time of two hours.

A perfect size for a day trip, Siena has a sense of calm and
openness that Florence, with its crocodiles of coach parties,
often lacks. Busloads rarely impinge on your wandering of the
ancient twisting streets and you may even find yourself alone in
one of the city squares during the afternoon closing period. The
heart of the city is the touristy Piazza del Campo, bristling with
cafés that may not serve the most authentic food in town, but
which offer a good place for people-watching. A perfect spot for
a picnic lunch is the large Botanic Garden which, with its free
admission, is a welcome change from the constant shelling out in
Florence. A long street heads south from the bus terminus, lined
with shops. To the west, the winding streets lead to the Duomo
while to the south is the Botanic Garden. North and west of the
bus terminus is the Piazza San Domenico and its huge monastery.
Nightlife here is a fairly quiet affair – families eat late and make an
evening of it. There are several bars in town aimed at the tourist
market, a couple with live music at weekends. Look for Maudit in
Vicolo dello Fortuna or the Tea Room, at the bottom of the steps
in Via dei Malcontenti, open nightly until 03.00.

The very helpful tourist office is in Piazza del Campo 56 ☎ 0577
280551 ⓦ www.terresiena.it

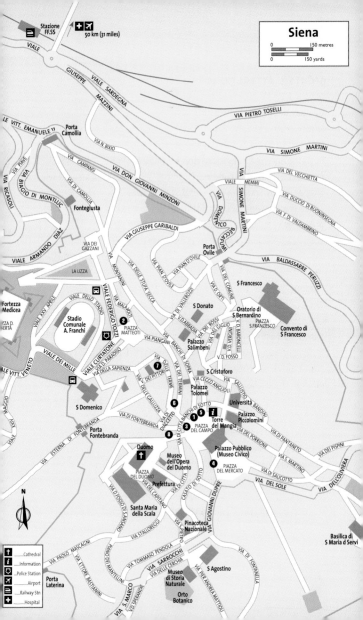

SIGHTS & ATTRACTIONS

Basilica di San Domenico

Mostly 20th-century restoration work, this monastery of the Dominican order is noteworthy for having been the place where St Catherine had her visions and bore the stigmata. Her head is encased in a marble tabernacle on the altar. Frescoes around the chapel are by Sodoma and show St Catherine in a state of ecstasy. There is a contemporary painting of her in the church by Giovanni di Stefano.

ⓐ Piazza San Domenico ⓣ 0577 28901 ⓛ 07.00–18.30 May–Oct, 09.00–18.00 Nov–Apr

Duomo

The open plan for this 12th-century church was to be the biggest in Christendom. Work was well under way on the extension in the 14th century when the plague hit the city. What remains is perhaps just as fascinating as what might have been – the unfinished nave stands, looking like a demolition site to the southwest of the church. The earlier Gothic building is covered by a black and white marble façade, designed in part by Giovanni Pisano (and currently covered up by massive restoration and cleaning works). Inside, the inlaid marble floors are also out of sight – covered up for most of the year, they get a special airing in autumn. Some big names worked on the inside of this church – Arnolfo di Cambio (Florence's Duomo), Nicolas Pisano and son (the pulpit) and an up-and-coming young sculptor called Michelangelo (statues of the saints on the Piccolomini altar). In the Libreria Piccolomini (1496), built to house

---

◗ *Siena's enormous Piazza del Campo*

the books of Pope Pius III (one of the shortest-sitting popes of all time at only 28 days), the frescoes are by Pinturicchio and his young assistant Raphael. Beside the church is the Baptistery, its exterior also unfinished, with its central font worked on by Lorenzo Ghiberti, Donatello and Jacopo.

ⓐ Piazza del Duomo ⓣ 0577 47321 ⓛ 10.00–19.30 Mon–Sat, 14.00–17.00 Sun (summer); 10.30–13.00, 14.00–18.00 Mon–Sat, 14.00–16.00 Sun (winter); admission charges for church, baptistery and for library

Fortezza Medicea

First they built it, then they knocked it down, then they built it again. The fortress was built in 1562 under orders of Charles V of Spain, demolished when Siena became independent of Spanish rule and then built again on the orders of Cosimo de' Medici after an 18-month-long siege by the Florentines. The square inside the fortress is called Piazza della Libertà, which is a strange kind of logic since it was built twice under the orders of foreign rulers, but in modern times it's a nice rural spot for an evening stroll with views over the city. Inside the fortress is the Enoteca Italiana, Italy's national wine cellar (ⓐ Piazza della Libertà ⓣ 0577 288497 ⓦ www.enotecaitaliana.it ⓛ 12.00–01.00 Tues–Sat, 12.00–20.00 Mon).

Orto Botanico

Two hectares (5 acres) of free garden to wander around in and eat your gorgeous picnic lunch, bought at one of the delicious bakeries and delicatessens in town.

ⓐ Via Matteoli 4 ⓣ 0577 232874 ⓛ 08.00–12.30, 14.30–17.30 Mon–Fri, 08.00–12.00 Sat

Palazzo Pubblico

This 14th-century building still functions as the City Hall but several of the rooms are open to the public. In the Sala del Mappa Mundo (map of the world room), there are two 14th-century paintings worth seeking out, both by Simone Martini. The *Maestà* shows the Virgin Mary as queen of heaven, surrounded by apostles, saints and angels. The other is a portrait of a mercenary soldier, Guidoriccio da Fogliano. In the adjacent chapel are 15th-century frescoes by Taddeo di Bartolo, depicting the *Life of the Virgin*. The 15th-century choir stalls here are also worth a look for their carved and inlaid panels, showing scenes from the Bible. The best works here, though, are in the Sala de Pace, where the 14th-century painter, Ambrogio Lorenzetti, has painted the *Allegory of Good and Bad Government*.
🅐 Piazza del Campo ☎ 0577 292263 🕓 10.00–17.30, until 19.00 summer; admission charge

Piazza del Campo & Torre del Mangia

What is it with powerful men and high towers? Siena's 14th-century rulers wanted the highest tower in Italy and so they got it, 102 m (335 ft) of brick-built bell tower, 503 steps which the bell ringers had to climb several times a day. Only 15 people at a time can climb the tower so you should book your place early if you want to see the views over the Piazza del Campo. This shell-shaped public place was originally a Roman forum, lying in the base of the surrounding hills and divided into nine segments, one for each of the medieval city's council members. The fountain at the north end dates back to 1408, its marble figures replaced with replicas in the 19th century.
🅐 Torre del Mangia, Piazza del Campo 🕓 10.00–19.00, until 23.00 July, Aug; admission charge ❶ Tickets from Museo Civico ticket office

CULTURE

Museo dell'Opera del Duomo

Built into the side aisle of the unfinished nave, this museum houses the Pisano sculptures from the façade of the building which were getting badly worn, as well as Duccio di Buoninsegna's *Pala della Maesta* (1308), which was originally the high altar of the Duomo. One side features the Madonna with saints, while the other has scenes from the life of Christ. From the loggia of the museum there are views over the city.

ⓐ Piazza del Duomo 8 ⓣ 0577 283048 ⓛ 09.00–19.30 Mar–Sept, 09.00–18.00 Oct–Feb; admission charge

Pinacoteca Nazionale

The artists of Siena followed a different path to the naturalistic style of Botticelli and company, and this can be seen in this museum and gallery set in the 14th-century Palazzo Buonsignori. There are over 1,500 works of art here and the Siena school is well represented with their characteristic gilded backgrounds, called *fondi d'oro*. Highlights are Lorenzetti's *Two Views* painted in the 14th century, and showing the rare use of landscape painting, and Pietro Domenico's *Adoration of the Shepherds* (1510) showing the typical *fondi d'oro* style.

ⓐ Via San Pietro 29 ⓣ 0577 281161 ⓛ 08.30–13.30; admission charge

Santa Maria della Scala

This erstwhile hospital for pilgrims, still in use in the 1980s, is now a museum with its original frescoes of hospital life still on the walls.

ⓞ *The unmistakeable striped marble facade of the Duomo*

Mostly home to temporary exhibitions (you should check what is on before paying the entrance fee), there is also a small archaeological museum.

ⓐ Piazza del Duomo 2 ⓣ 0577 224811

ⓦ www.santamariadellascala.com ⓛ 10.30–18.30 (summer); 10.30–16.30 (winter); admission charge

RETAIL THERAPY

The main roads through Banchi di Sopra and Via di Città is home to the best of the city's shops. Lots of familiar names here, especially along Banchi di Sopra – Benetton, Footlocker and Max Mara. Some local clothes shops include Extyn, Bloom and the department store UPIM, a bit downmarket but worth a browse. Mori in Banchi di Sopra has designer shoes, bags and jackets in leather and Yamamay (62–63, in the same street), has fashionable underwear. If you are in town on the right day, there is a general market that is fun to browse around on Wednesdays (08.00–13.00) along Piazza La Lizza, while an antiques market is held on some Sundays in the Piazza del Mercato.

Drago Rosso Artefacts from around the world – jumpers from Ecuador, tapestries from India, teapots, ethnic jewellery, interesting clothes. ⓐ Via dei Pellegrini 13 ⓣ 0577 285102 ⓛ 10.00–20.00

La Fabbrica delle Candel Siena Everything you can think of made of wax – flowers, dolphins, buddhas. Lovely candles, handmade and painted in the shop. ⓐ Via dei Pellegrini ⓣ 0577 236417 ⓦ www.lafabricadellecandele.com ⓛ 09.30–19.30 Mon–Wed, Fri & Sat, 10.00–19.30 Sun

La Fontana della Fruta Fresh fruit, gorgeous cakes, nuts, cheeses, things in olive oil, salamis, bread, filled rolls. ⓐ Via delle Terme 65–67 ⓘ 0577 40422 ⓒ 08.00–20.00 Mon–Sat

Mazzuoli Pretty inexpensive shoes and bags. ⓐ Piazza de Campo 25 ⓒ 10.00–15.00, 15.30–19.30

Morbidi More than just a delicatessen shop, this has stacks of pickled and bottled goodies, cooked meats, vegetables swimming in oil, wine and lots more for a picnic lunch. ⓐ Via Banchi di Sopra 73 ⓘ 0577 280268 ⓒ 09.00–20.00 Mon–Sat

La Bottega dei Sapori Antichi Delicatessen with lots of good things for a picnic lunch. For good bread, go next door to Forno Independenza (09.00–13.00). ⓐ Via delle Terme 39/41 ⓒ 08.00–20.00 Mon–Sat

Swarovski Lovely glass things – delicate jewellery, ornaments, objects d'art. Prices to match. ⓐ Via di Città 11 ⓘ 0577 44572 ⓒ 09.30–17.30 Mon–Fri

Tezennis Some attractive underwear. ⓐ Via di Città 12 ⓒ 09.30–19.30 Mon–Sat, 15.30–19.30 Sun

TAKING A BREAK

Fiorella £ ❶ Tiny coffee shop, one or two seats, with the emphasis on coffee. ⓐ Via di Città 13 ⓘ 0577 271255 ⓒ 07.00–19.00

La Cascina £ ❷ Good all-round cake, coffee and aperitif shop, close to the bus terminus. More substantial dishes of pasta and ciabatta

for lunch. ⓐ Piazza G Matteoti ⓣ 0577 283282 ⓛ 07.00–20.00
Mon–Sat, 07.30–20.00 Sun

La Costarella £ ❸ *Gelaterie* with the usual array of flavours, cakes
and coffee. ⓐ Via di Città 33 ⓛ 08.30–21.00 Fri–Wed, until 24.00
summer

La Finestra £ ❹ Busy, bright, well-kept restaurant with tables
outside in the market square. Usual menu of salads, pasta –
including *pici*, the traditional pasta of Siena – some interesting main
courses and carpaccio. No menu in English, so aimed largely at the
local market. ⓐ Piazza del Mercato 14 ⓣ 0577 42093 ⓛ 12.00–15.00,
19.00–22.00 Mon–Sat

Nannini £ ❺ Familiar café with a branch in Florence. Cakes and
rolls, good cappuccino, huge buffet lunch from 12.00. Stand at the
bar for an inexpensive coffee and cake or sit down for the waitress
service and pay more. ⓐ Via Banchi di Sopra 24 ⓣ 0577 236009
ⓛ 07.30–21.00

AFTER DARK

Restaurants
Enoteca I Terzi ££ ❻ Basically a wine bar in a red-brick, candle-lit
room. Come for lunch or dinner, and stay for the wine. Small menu
up on a blackboard changes each day. ⓐ Via dei Termini 7 ⓣ 0577
44329 ⓦ www.enotecaiterzi.it ⓛ 11.00–16.00, 18.30–01.00 Mon–Sat

Compagnia dei Vinattieri ££–£££ ❼ Stylish reflective basement
dining room with high stone arches, tastefully decorated and a

THE SIENESE PALIO

If you are in Tuscany on 2 July or 16 August, you, along with thousands of others, will probably be at Tuscany's most famous festival in the Piazza del Campo. The enormous square fills up to breaking point and vast sums change hands with those people lucky enough to own a window with a view of the piazza. The 17 districts of the city choose their horse and rider by drawing lots and several pre-race races take place to choose the entries. The race starts at about 19.00 and the three laps of the Campo take about 90 seconds. Jockeys ride bareback on the horses and rivalry is real and fierce; horses occasionally break legs and have to be put down and the winners brag about their victory for the following year.

● *The thrilling action of the Palio*

welcoming atmosphere. Try the pasta with wild boar, ravioli with pigeon or rabbit with olives, traditional Tuscan fare. A pleasant evening that won't damage your plastic. ⓐ Via delle Terme 79 ⓣ 0577 236568 ⓦ www.vinattieri.net ⓛ 11.00–19.00

Da Mugolone ££–£££ ❽ Classy, quiet, spacious yet affordable. Classic Sienese dishes such as fried calf brain, pheasant cooked in foil and fried rabbit. Less adventurous visitors could go for the beef with garlic and rosemary. Exciting desserts. ⓐ Via dei Pellegrini 8 ⓣ 0577 283235 ⓛ 12.30–22.00 Mon–Wed, Fri, Sat, 12.30–15.00 Sun

ACCOMMODATION

Colleverde £ Campsite 3 km (2 miles) outside the city with lots of facilities – bar, café, pool, shop etc. ⓐ Strada Scacciapensieri 47 ⓣ 0577 280044, closed Nov–Mar

Antica Torre ££ Possibly the best value in town, this small hotel is in a renovated 16th-century tower. Lots of atmosphere and close to all the sights. Rooftop views. Only eight rooms so book well in advance. ⓐ Via di Fieravecchi 7 ⓣ 0577 222255 ⓦ www.anticatorresiena.it

Santa Caterina ££ Close to the city walls this is a fairly modern building – 18th century. Only 22 rooms, individually decorated. Garden and terrace with lovely views. ⓐ Via Enea Silvio Piccolomini 7 ⓣ 0577 221105 ⓦ www.hscsiena.it

---

◗ *Palazzo Vecchio*

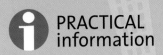

PRACTICAL information

Directory

GETTING THERE
By air

For a short stay most people arriving from the UK will find flying the quickest and most convenient way to travel, either from Gatwick to the small Amerigo Vespucci airport or into Pisa's Galileo Galilei which has considerably more connections to cities in the UK via

○ *If you do hire a car, the Tuscan scenery is breathtaking*

easyJet and Ryanair as well as Alitalia, British Airways and Meridiana flights. There are no direct intercontinental flights.

Alitalia ☎ 055 27881 ⓦ www.alitalia.it
BA ☎ 199 712266 / 050 501838 (Pisa) ⓦ www.britishairways.com
easyJet ☎ 848 887766 ⓦ www.easyjet.co.uk
Meridiana ☎ 055 2302334 ⓦ www.meridiana.it
Ryanair ☎ 050 503770 ⓦ www.ryanair.com

By rail
The UK is connected to Florence from Waterloo Station via the Eurostar, changing at Paris. Timetables and fares are available at:
Rail Europe ⓦ www.raileurope.co.uk (UK)
ⓦ www.eurorailways.com (US)
The Man in Seat 61 ⓦ www.seat61.com
Thomas Cook European Rail Timetable
ⓦ www.thomascookpublishing.com ☎ 01733 416477 (UK)
1800 322 3834 (US)
Eurostar ☎ 08705 186186 ⓦ www.eurostar.com

By road
There is little point to a trip to Florence by car unless you intend to drive around Tuscany. Car drivers will need a Green Card and their registration documents. Buses connect Florence with all major European cities and coach fares are generally lower than the equivalent journey by train although, of course, they take longer. National Express Eurolines operate a service from London Victoria in conjunction with Lazzi Express which takes approximately 28 hours and involves two changes of bus.
ⓦ www.nationalexpress.com

ENTRY FORMALITIES

Visa requirements

EU, US, Canadian, Australian and New Zealand citizens do not
need visas for stays of up to three months. Visitors are supposed
to register with the police within three days of arrival. This formality
is carried out during your registration at your accommodation.
South African visitors require a visa.

Customs

EU citizens do not have to declare goods imported or exported
as long as they are for their personal use and they have arrived
from within the EU. For non-EU citizens the following import
restrictions apply:
400 cigarettes or 200 small cigars or 100 cigars or 500 g of tobacco
1 litre of spirits or 2 litres of fortified wine
50 grams of perfume
€10,000 cash

MONEY

Italy is a member of the European Union, with the euro is
the currency. This has seven banknotes: €5, €10, €20, €50, €100,
€200 and €500. Coins come in denominations of €1, €2 and
1, 2, 5, 10, 20 and 50 cent. There are 24-hour cashpoints located
outside most banks, and these will accept cards with Cirrus and
Maestro symbols. You can also withdraw cash using Visa, Access and
MasterCard. The daily limit at these cash machines is often as
little as €250, and your bank will make a charge for credit card
use. Bank opening hours are 08.20–13.20, 14.35–15.35 Mon–Fri.
They close on public holidays and work shorter hours on the days
before public holidays. Most banks have double security doors –

press the buzzer to get through the first door and wait in the vestibule until the next door opens.

Florence and Pisa airports have cash exchange machines where you feed in uncrumpled notes in your currency and get euros out. The exchange rate is displayed on the machine.

Sterling and dollar users might want to consider traveller's cheques, which can be exchanged in banks or bureaux de change or some hotels for a commission.

Bureaux de change open out of banking hours, but will probably charge for each exchange you make and their exchange rate may be less beneficial to you than a bank. Post offices (*ufficio postale*) charge €2.50 for all transactions, regardless of how much. The Thomas Cook Bureau (ⓐ Lungarno Acciaiuoli 4/8r ⓣ 055 290278) is open on Sundays and doesn't charge for cash exchange with Visa and MasterCard.

HEALTH, SAFETY & CRIME

EU citizens are entitled to the same medical care as Italians, although you must bring a European Health Insurance Card (EHIC) with you. The website for ordering these cards is ⓦ www.ehic.org.uk This replaces the old E111 form. To consult with a GP you must go to the nearest Azienda Sanitaria di Firenze or public health centre (your hotel will advise where that is), taking your EHIC with you. Medicine and tests may cost extra and the EHIC will not cover repatriation or other costs involved in getting home in an emergency. For this you must take out separate medical insurance cover. If you have to spend time in hospital you are expected to provide towels, eating utensils and toilet paper. Non-EU nationals are entitled to free emergency medical care but should take out medical insurance for all other situations. Pharmacies (*farmacia*) can be identified by a green or red cross, and staff will advise on non-prescription drugs for minor illnesses. Opening hours are 08.30–13.00, 16.00–18.00 Mon–Fri, 08.00–13.00 Sat but operate a duty roster so that there is always one available. The roster is usually posted up by the door. A website for health-related travel advice for British citizens is Ⓦ www.dh.gov.uk/travellers

HEALTH INFORMATION

Ⓦ www.doh.gov.uk/travellers and Ⓦ www.fco.gov.uk/travel websites for health and travel advice from the British government

Ⓦ www.cdc.gov/travel and Ⓦ www.healthfinder.com websites for American travellers

Ⓦ www.travelhealth.co.uk useful tips and information.

Ⓦ www.who.int/en World Health Organization

Ⓦ www.tripprep.com Travel Health Online

Ⓦ www.brookes.ac.uk/worldwise basic travel information on countries

Dentists are not covered by the EHIC and are more expensive than in Britain.

Italians tend to drink bottled water, although tap water is safe to drink. There are no inoculations necessary for a visit to Italy, although mosquitoes can be a pest, particularly for women. Carry mosquito repellent, especially if you are leaving the city. In spring and summer sunburn can be a problem, so apply sun cream, wear a hat and in the heat of the day stay indoors if you are at all sensitive. Carry water with you.

Street crime is a factor to take into account in the city. Pickpockets and moped-riding bag snatchers operate in the tourist areas, on buses and at the railway station. Simple common sense precautions should help keep them at bay – wear a shoulder bag across your chest and keep it fastened and in sight at all times. Do not keep your wallet in a back pocket or in an obtrusive lump in your front pocket. Carry only as much cash as you need for the day and keep other valuables in your hotel. The police are ever present at the major tourist spots.

There are different kinds of policemen, but in an emergency any of them will help. The people in blue uniforms and white hats (white uniforms in summer), are the Vigili Urbani – they are traffic police. A similar uniform with a red stripe in the trousers belongs to the carabinieri, whose area of expertise is speeding and street crime. La Polizia are dressed in blue with white belts, and work on more serious crime. If you are robbed you must report the matter to the police within 24 hours and obtain a statement. For details of what to do in an emergency, see page 154.

OPENING HOURS

Check opening hours of sights and shops that you intend to visit before making your journey. Opening hours in Florence are Byzantine and also flexible, but the following generalisations can be tentatively applied:

Shops: Department stores, shoe shops and the like open at 09.00 and close at 13.00. Not for them, the long working day. Later, they open at 15.30 and close at 19.30. They generally remain closed on Monday mornings. No one in the retail trade hates Mondays in Florence. Supermarkets, grocers and markets open earlier and close at 13.00 and can reopen at 17.00, except on Wednesdays when they remain closed after 13.00. All shops generally close on Saturday afternoons in summer, and shops and markets may close for three weeks around 15 August.

Museums: These have their own sets of opening hours but generally open only in the mornings and are closed on Mondays. Private museums often open longer hours into the afternoon.

TOILETS

Bars allow passers by to use their toilets, which is fortunate since public toilets are a rarity. There are toilets in the underpass by the railway station and in Palazzo Vecchio and Palazzo Pitti, in Sant'Ambrogio market and in Piazzale Michelangelo.

CHILDREN

Italy is a very child-oriented country and Florence is no exception to this. Restaurants welcome children, have smoke-free areas by law, and some offer child menus. Parents should be aware of the heat of the sun, even in spring, but beyond that no special health precautions need be taken. Disposable nappies, baby milk and little jars of baby food are readily available in supermarkets. Bring any medication such as child aspirin, inhalers, anti-histamine with you. Your main problem in bringing children to the city is to be aware that Renaissance paintings and ancient architecture may not be their idea of a good day out. There are, however, places where the offspring can have fun and all parents will know the benefits of a happy child.

- **Giardino di Bóboli** Fountains, grottoes, an amphitheatre and summer shows (see page 98).

- **La Specola** Wax models of dissected bodies for the yuck factor that children love so much (see page 101).

- **Mondobimbo Inflatables** Bouncy castles in Piazza della Libertà ⏱ June–Aug

- **Museo de Ragazzi** Dedicated to the childlike, this museum has puppet shows, dressing up corners, workshops, medieval characters to talk to and more. Workshops conducted in English on some Saturdays. ⓐ Palazzo Vecchio, Piazza della Signoria ⏱ 09.30–13.00, 14.00–19.00; admission charge

- **Museo Leonardo da Vinci** Many of Leonardo's drawings are brought to life size with hands-on bits and pieces, his aeroplanes, tanks and more. ⓐ Via dei Serri 66–68r ⏱ 10.00–19.00

- **Parco delle Cascine** West of the city, bordering the river, is the city's largest park with lots of space to run around and a kiosk hiring line skates. ⓐ Nr Ponte della Victoria

- **Piazzale Michelangelo** More climbing for amazing views and ice cream at the top (see page 102).

- **The Duomo** Climb to the top to wear out children and get great views (see page 84).

COMMUNICATIONS
Phone
Making phone calls from Italy is an expensive business. Phone boxes take phone cards (*schede telefoniche*), which can be bought at news

stands or *tabacchi*. Also available in these places and cheaper are the phone cards where you dial an 0800 number and tap in your code. These can be used both for domestic and international calls. Hotel phone rates can be astronomical. Public phone boxes can be found in the big public squares and in bars. Rates are lower after 18.30 and cheaper still after 22.00. Look for a sign with a red telephone receiver inside a red circle.

Telephoning Florence

The international code for Italy is 00 39 (from UK) or 011 39 (from the US). The code for Florence is 055, Pisa 050, Siena 0577.

TELEPHONING ABROAD

Dial 00, the international access code, followed by your country code and then the area code minus the initial zero, followed by the number itself.

UK country code: 44
Ireland: 353
France: 33
Germany: 49
USA: 1
Canada: 1
Australia: 61
New Zealand: 64
South Africa: 27

Post

When sending letters most people use *poste priorità*, which is a little more expensive and needs a special sticker and has to be put in special boxes either marked *poste priorità* or coloured blue. Regular post boxes are red and have two slots – one for letters within the city (*per la Città*), and one for all other destinations. Stamps and stickers can be bought in tobacconists, which have a T sign, as well as post offices (*ufficio postale*). Opening hours are 08.15–13.30 Mon–Fri, until 12.30 Sat. Post offices are located at ❸ Via Pellicceria 3 ❶ 055 281156, ❸ Via Cavour 71A, San Marco ❶ 055 463501 and ❸ Via Barbadori 37r, Oltrarno ❶ 055 288175

Internet

Internet access is relatively easy – there are Internet shops around the city and many hotels have access points for their guests. Internet time runs at about €5 an hour. ID is always required. Plugging in your laptop might be difficult in older hotels, since some phone plugs in Florence are different to those used in Britain and the US. Internet shops are located at:

Internet Train ❸ Via de'Conti 23r, San Lorenzo 🕒 10.00–24.00

Virtual Office ❸ Via Faenza 49r, San Lorenzo 🕒 10.00–24.00 Mon–Wed, 10.00–01.00 Thur–Sat, 12.00–01.00 Sun

ADDRESSES

Not for Florence the simple logic of a series of street numbers starting at the beginning and going up as the street progresses. The city has two sets of numbers for every street. Businesses, shops, restaurants have one set of numbers, recognisable by a red number on the building, and written on letters with an 'r' following it, while residential addresses are black and have no following letter.

ELECTRICITY

Electrical current in Italy is 220V AC and plugs are two pin, round-pronged. Adapters can be bought at the airport.

TRAVELLERS WITH DISABILITIES

Recent legislation means that wheelchair users will have a much less stressful time in Florence, although the rules apply only to new buildings. Most modern hotels will have ramps and lifts, as do museums, while the most recently bought buses have lowering ramps. The few trains with wheelchair access have the wheelchair logo marked. Access to Santa Novella train station is at the east or north side, and you can ring in advance for assistance (📞 055 2352275). A booklet is available from tourist offices, with information on accessibility of various sights. You can also check at 🌐 www.comune.fi.it. Owners of a disabled driver sticker can use pedestrianised areas of the city and there are adequate disabled parking bays around the city. Florence and Pisa airports have disabled access toilets, as does Santa Novella station.

TOURIST INFORMATION

ENIT 🌐 www.enit.it will send out information packs on Florence and specialist holidays on request at the website.
🅰 Via Cavour 1r, San Lorenzo 📞 055 29082 🕐 08.00–19.15 Mon–Sat
🅰 Piazza della Stazione 4a, Santa Maria Novella 📞 055 212245
🕐 08.30–13.00, 15.30–19.00 Mon–Sat, 09.00–13.30 Sun

Tourist Help is available from three police vans stationed in Piazza della Repubblica, one in Via Calzaiuoli (often parked in Piazza della Signoria) and one at the southern entrance to the Ponte Vecchio. They will give directions and help. 🕐 08.00–19.00

FURTHER READING

Art

Lives of the Artists Giorgio Vasari, Penguin. You've seen his art, now read the stories behind it.

Prisoners of Art: Florence in 2 Days for adults and children. Firenzi Musei. Entertaining book about Florence's art for children.

Cookery

Genaro's Italian Year Contaldo Genaro, Headline. A season by season guide to Italian cookery.

Just Like Mamma used to Make More Italian recipes.

Passione Contaldo Genaro, Headline. Southern Italian recipes.

The Silver Spoon Ed. Linda Doeser, Phaidon. The original Italian cookery bible from the 1950s, updated and translated into English for the first time.

General

Medici Money Tim Parks, Profile Books. The history of the Medici family and their relationship with money.

The Stones of Florence, Mary McCarthy, Penguin. Travel writing about the city.

 PRACTICAL INFORMATION

Useful phrases

Although English is spoken in many tourist locations in Florence, these words and phrases may come in handy. See also the phrases for specific situations in other parts of this book.

English	Italian	Approx. pronunciation
BASICS		
Yes	Sì	See
No	No	Noh
Please	Per favore	Perr fahvawreh
Thank you	Grazie	Grahtsyeh
Hello	Salve	Sahlveh
Goodbye	Arrivederci	Arreevehderrchee
Excuse me	Scusi	Skoozee
Sorry	Scusi	Skoozee
That's okay	Va bene	Vah behneh
To	A	Ah
From	Da	Dah
I don't speak Italian	Non parlo italiano	Nawn parrlaw itahlyahnaw
Do you speak English?	Parla inglese?	Parrla eenglehzeh?
Good morning	Buon giorno	Booawn geeyawrnaw
Good afternoon	Buon pomeriggio	Booawn pawmehreehdjaw
Good evening	Buonasera	Booawnah sehrah
Goodnight	Buonanotte	Booawnah nawtteh
My name is …	Mi chiamo …	Mee kyahmaw …
DAYS & TIMES		
Monday	Lunedì	Loonehdee
Tuesday	Martedì	Marrtehdee
Wednesday	Mercoledì	Merrcawlehdee
Thursday	Giovedì	Jawvehdee
Friday	Venerdì	Venerrdee
Saturday	Sabato	Sahbahtaw
Sunday	Domenica	Dawmehneeca
Morning	Mattino	Mahtteenaw
Afternoon	Pomeriggio	Pawmehreedjaw
Evening	Sera	Sehra
Night	Notte	Notteh
Yesterday	Ieri	Yeree

English	Italian	Approx. pronunciation
Today	Oggi	Odjee
Tomorrow	Domani	Dawmahnee
What time is it?	Che ore sono?	Keh awreh sawnaw?
It is ...	Sono le ...	Sawnaw leh ...
09.00	Nove	Noveh
Midday	Mezzogiorno	Metsawjorrnaw
Midnight	Mezzanotte	Metsanotteh

NUMBERS

One	Uno	Oonaw
Two	Due	Dweh
Three	Tre	Treh
Four	Quattro	Kwahttraw
Five	Cinque	Cheenkweh
Six	Sei	Say
Seven	Sette	Setteh
Eight	Otto	Ottaw
Nine	Nove	Noveh
Ten	Dieci	Dyehchee
Eleven	Undici	Oondeechee
Twelve	Dodici	Dawdeechee
Twenty	Venti	Ventee
Fifty	Cinquanta	Cheenkwahnta
One hundred	Cento	Chentaw

MONEY

I would like to change these traveller's cheques/this currency	Vorrei cambiare questi assegni turistici/ questa valuta	Vawrray cahmbyahreh kwestee assenee tooree-steechee/kwesta vahloota
Where is the nearest ATM?	Dov'è il bancomat più vicino?	Dawveh eel bankomaht pyoo veecheenaw?
Do you accept credit cards?	Accettate carte di credito?	Achetahteh kahrrteh dee krehdeehtaw?

SIGNS & NOTICES

Airport	Aeroporto	Ahaerrhawpawrrtaw
Railway station	Stazione ferroviaria	Stahtsyawneh ferrawvyarya
Platform	Binario	Binahriaw
Smoking/ non-smoking	Per fumatori/ non fumatori	Perr foomahtawree/ non foomahtawree
Toilets	Gabinetti	Gabinettee
Ladies/Gentlemen	Signore/Signori	Seenyawreh/Seenyawree
Subway	Metropolitana	Metrawpawleetahna

Emergencies

EMERGENCY NUMBERS
Ambulance (Ambulanza) ☎ 118
Fire (Vigili del Fuoco) ☎ 115
Police (English speaking helpline) ☎ 112
Car breakdown ☎ 803 116 (connects to Automobile Club d'Italia)
Traffic police ☎ 05 32831

Lost or stolen credit cards
American Express ☎ 06 72282
American Express Gold Card ☎ 06 722807385
Diners Club ☎ 800 864064
Eurocard, MasterCard, Visa ☎ 800 018548

Accident and Emergency departments are open 24 hours, or call 118. This number will also provide you with the address of doctors on emergency call out. The following hospitals have A&E departments (*pronto soccorso*):

Santa Maria Nuova 🄰 Piazza Santa Maria Nuova 1 ☎ 055 27581. This is the most central hospital in Florence and has a 24-hour pharmacy.

Ospedale Meyer (children) 🄰 Via Luca Giordano 13 ☎ 055 56621 🄝 Bus: 11, 17

Ospedale di Careggi ☎ 055 4277111 🄝 Bus: 2, 8, 14c

▶ *An overview of Florence's Campanile and Duomo*

Association of Hospital Volunteers (AVO) is an organisation which will, if needed, provide translation services in hospitals ☎ 055 4250126 (24 hours).

MEDICAL SERVICES

If you are an EU citizen, to see a GP when it isn't an emergency you can go to the state health centre (Azienda Sanitaria di Firenze) of the area where you are staying (your hotel will know where that is), taking your EHIC card. ASLs generally open from ⏰ 09.00–13.00, 14.00–19.00 Mon–Fri.

Dr Stephen Kerr ➋ Via Porta Rossa 1 ☎ 055 288055 has a private surgery, speaks English and will charge €40, plus for a consultation. Drop in clinic 15.00–17.00 Mon–Fri.

Associated Medical Studio ➌ Via Lorenzo il Magnifico ☎ 055 475411 (24 hours) will send out English-speaking doctors on request. Fees between €80 and €100.

EMERGENCY PHRASES

Help! Aiuto! *Ahyootaw!*   **Fire!** Al fuoco! *Ahl fooawcaw!*
Stop! Ferma! *Fairmah!*

Call an ambulance/a doctor/the police/the fire service!
Chiamate un'ambulanza/un medico/la polizia/i pompieri!
Kyahmahteh oon ahmboolahntsa/oon mehdeecaw/la pawleetsya/ee pompee-ehree!

LOST PROPERTY

Ufficio Oggetti ⓐ Ritrovati Circondari 19 ☎ 055 3283942
🕓 09.00–12.00 Mon–Sat Ⓝ Bus: 23. For items lost about town.

Taxis

If you lose something in a taxi, you can phone the cab company and
give the number of the cab. After a time drivers will hand things in
to the police station ☎ 055 212290

Trains

Platform 16, next to left luggage ☎ 055 2352190 🕓 06.00–24.00

CONSULATES & EMBASSIES

There are no embassies in Florence although there are some
consulates who can give advice.

British Consulate ⓐ Lungarno Cosine 2 ☎ 055 284133 🕓 09.30–12.30,
14.30–16.30 Mon–Fri, out of hours you will be directed to an
emergency number.

US Consulate ⓐ Lungarno A Vespucci 38 ☎ 055 298276
🕓 09.00–12.30, 14.30–15.30 Mon–Fri, out of hours you will be
directed to an emergency number.

South African Consulate ⓐ Piazza dei Salter Elli 1 ☎ 055 281863

Embassies

Australia ⓐ Via Aleksandra 215 Rome ☎ 06 852 721
Canada ⓐ Via GB de Rossi 27, Rome ☎ 06 445 981
Ireland ⓐ Piazza Campitelli 3, Rome ☎ 06 697 9121
New Zealand ⓐ Via Zara 26, Rome ☎ 06 441 7171

INDEX

ACKNOWLEDGEMENTS & FEEDBACK

The publishers would like to thank the following for supplying their copyright photographs for this book: Pictures Colour Library pp 17, 21, 29, 31, 40–41, 46, 91, 107, 111, 117, 123, 129, 132, 137, 140, 155; Robert Harding World Imagery p 12; Timothy Sewter pp 5, 103, 139; all the rest Pat Levy.

Copy editor: Natasha Reed
Proofreader: Lynn Bresler

Send your thoughts to
books@thomascook.com

- **Found a great bar, club, shop or must-see sight that we don't feature?**
- **Like to tip us off about any information that needs updating?**
- **Want to tell us what you love about this handy little guidebook and more importantly how we can make it even handier?**

Then here's your chance to tell all! Send us ideas, discoveries and recommendations today and then look out for your valuable input in the next edition of this title. As an extra 'thank you' from Thomas Cook Publishing, you'll be automatically entered into our exciting monthly prize draw.

Send an email to the above address (stating the book's title) or write to: CitySpots Project Editor, Thomas Cook Publishing, PO Box 227, The Thomas Cook Business Park, Unit 18, Coningsby Road, Peterborough PE3 8SB, UK.